EVERGREEN PILOT BOOKS

Chief Editor

A. Norman Jeffares

Advisory Editors

David Daiches   C. P. Snow

EZRA POUND

EZRA POUND

G. S. Fraser

GROVE PRESS, INC.
NEW YORK

First published by Oliver and Boyd Ltd
Edinburgh, Scotland, 1960

Library of Congress Catalog number 61-6595

First Evergreen Edition 1961
Second Printing

Manufactured in Great Britain

CONTENTS

ACKNOWLEDGMENTS

I am grateful to Mr Ezra Pound himself for permission for all quotations from his works.

Acknowledgment is due to Faber and Faber Ltd, publishers of the following works by Ezra Pound: *Selected Poems*, 1928; *Personae: Collected Shorter Poems of Ezra Pound*, 1952; *The Cantos of Ezra Pound*, 1954; *Literary Essays*, 1954. Also to New Directions, publishers of the following American editions: *The Cantos of Ezra Pound*, 1949; *Personae: The Collected Poems of Ezra Pound*, 1950.

Acknowledgments are also due to the following authors and publishers for permission to quote from the works indicated: Chatto and Windus Ltd (F. R. Leavis, *New Bearings in English Poetry*); The Clarendon Press (introduction to *The Oxford Book of Modern Verse*); Faber and Faber Ltd (T. S. Eliot, *Collected Poems 1909–15*); Mr Robert Graves and Cassell and Co. Ltd (Robert Graves, *The Crowning Privilege*); Mr Robert Graves and Hamish Hamilton Ltd (Robert Graves, *The Common Asphodel*); *The Hudson Review* Inc. (article by Roy Harvey Pearce); Methuen and Co. Ltd (Wyndham Lewis, *Time and Western Man*); Peter Owen Ltd (Louise Bogan, *Selected Criticism*); University of Chicago Press (Hannah Arendt, *The Human Condition*).

The photograph on the front cover is reproduced by permission of the Keystone Press Agency.

G. S. F.

ABBREVIATED TITLES
BY WHICH EZRA POUND'S WORKS AND THOSE OF SOME OF HIS CRITICS ARE CITED IN THE TEXT

C.	=	*The Cantos of Ezra Pound.* 1954 edn.
L.E.	=	*The Literary Essays of Ezra Pound*
P.	=	*Personae: Collected Shorter Poems of Ezra Pound.* 1952 edn.
S.P.	=	*Selected Poems of Ezra Pound, with an introduction by T. S. Eliot*
H.R.	=	*The Hudson Review,* Autumn 1959
N.B.E.P.	=	F. R. Leavis, *New Bearings in English Poetry*
O.M.V.	=	*The Oxford Book of Modern Verse*
S.C.	=	Louise Bogan, *Selected Criticism*
T.W.M.	=	Wyndham Lewis, *Time and Western Man*

CHAPTER I

THE MAN AND HIS IDEAS

Ezra Pound is the most morally, aesthetically, and culturally controversial literary figure of this century. He is the Founding Father of the "modern movement" in Anglo-American poetry, Yeats and Eliot respected him as a technical adviser; yet a fine English poet like Robert Graves considers him a complete charlatan, and a fine American poet and critic like Yvor Winters considers him an influential poet of the third rank, an equivalent, say, to the Masefield of *The Everlasting Mercy*. One of his great creative passions, throughout his life, has been for translation; Eliot, again, says that he has, in English, for our time, created Chinese poetry; a number of academic critics have asserted that he does not properly know any of the languages he has translated from, and that he handles his own Anglo-American language in a coarse and vulgar fashion.

His most ambitious long poem, the *Cantos*, has been hailed as the only English achievement in the epic manner, and on the epic scale, since *Paradise Lost*, and also denounced as a pedantic rag-bag. His political and economic ideas, which led to his broadcasting from Italy during the war when his native country, the United States, was fighting against Italy, have been seen both as springing from some deep fundamental insight and from an unbalanced mind. He has been seen as one of the most subtle and complex of modern poets, and also as a poet of childlike *naïveté*. He has been regarded as an egotistic self-advertiser and also as the most modest and generous of men. His work as a whole can be seen as having an

almost Mark-Twainish American naturalness, or as a
series of exercises in artifice and affectation. He can be
seen as a man who renewed the "tradition," when both
English and American poetry were in the doldrums, or on
the other hand as a man who has set dozens of young
poets off on the wrong track. He can be seen as a Fascist,
as a bitter reactionary, or as a large-hearted Jeffersonian
radical whom Fascism took in. To many of his country-
men, during and after the Second World War, he seemed
a traitor; but it is also possible to see him as a very centrally American poet, strangely combining the traditions
of Longfellow (a great-uncle of his), Whitman, and
Henry James. In the hum and buzz of discussion that
arises when his name is mentioned, only one thing is
certain: he is not a poet to be ignored.

I am writing this little plain man's guide to Pound
partly because Pound's writings in prose and verse have
stirred, interested, delighted, exasperated me for about
thirty years; I am now forty-five, I came across the little
volume of his *Selected Poems*, published in England with
an introduction by T. S. Eliot, when I was fifteen. And
if Pound had not had the gift, which is one of his great
gifts, of stirring curiosity, I might have remained completely unaware, for instance, of Cavalcanti, Propertius,
early American history, great patches of Italian Renaissance history, Ovid's *Metamorphoses*, Chinese poetry, the
Japanese *haiku*, the English Pre-Raphaelites and Decadents, and a whole far wider range of foci in time and
space that are now alive to me. To Pound, even more
than to Eliot, we owe our contemporary sense of an enor-
mous variety of the literary modes and devices and
achievements of a dozen cultures as being spread about
before us like (in a phrase which Donald Davie, borrow-
ing it from André Malraux, uses about Pound) an
"imaginary museum." He has helped to give content to
the notion, which tends in all of us to be either very
vague or very provincially biased, of "human culture."

My interest in Pound has been also intensified by having had a life-pattern, in some ways, not unlike his. I served during the war in Egypt and Eritrea; I spent an intensive three months in South America, shortly after the war; and a little later spent eighteen months teaching and learning in Japan. When Pound writes about Fascism, or Confucianism, or about the aesthetics of Chinese or Japanese poetry, he therefore writes about topics which are not completely notional to me but with which I have a certain actual and direct, though obviously fragmentary and imperfect, acquaintance. That acquaintance sometimes helps me to judge the wisdom, or unwisdom, of what Pound says.

Pound praises Mussolini, and by implication the general ethos of Italian Fascism; and I remember the story of the high Italian Fascist official who was found, when the British forces entered Asmara in 1941, to be hoarding hundreds of tins of powdered milk, desperately needed in semi-siege conditions by mothers with young babies. Pound similarly praises Confucianism, a system essentially of deference and self-sacrifice within the large family group, or in one's place of work; a system which deals with relations to inferiors and superiors, but not to equals; with duties to those within what might be called the "clan," but not to strangers. An old woman once fell in a faint in a crowded Tokyo street, and it was my wife, not any Japanese, who managed to get an ambulance; the Japanese hurrying by on the other side had their own old grandmothers to look after, and were not extending their responsibilities. And the Confucian system of deference also means that Socratic discourse, free and frank discourse between equals, is in Japan almost impossible. A junior never questions the ideas of a senior. On things like Fascism and Confucianism, Pound seems to me to go by the book, not by any really sharp and revealing experience of how the thing works in practice.

It is right to begin this study with such a statement

both of how much one owes to Pound, for extending one's
curiosity, and of how much, whenever one sees ideas of
which he has expressed approval working out in practice,
one finds oneself disagreeing with him. He started off as
an almost purely aesthetic poet, in some of the later
Cantos he has become an almost purely didactic poet. His
"wisdom," what the didacticism embodies, is a queer
thing. It is a mixture of American cracker-barrel shrewd-
ness (Gertrude Stein called Pound "a village explainer"),
the general idea not only exemplified by but often rather
dissolved in the sometimes not immediately obviously
relevant anecdote, and of the appeal to authority, what
Adams, Jefferson, Confucius, even Tallulah's father
Senator Bankhead, said. There is of course a great fundamental modesty in this approach; we rarely get even
in the most didactic later *Cantos* something that just
Pound himself said, right off the cuff.

It is better, I think, to start off in this way by facing
some of the hostile reactions which Pound's ideas, his
personality, his personal history arouse, rather than to
dodge round these hostile reactions, evasively and
politely, all through this book. The best way of confront-
ing these hostile reactions is, I think, by pointing out that
very generous emotions lie behind what seem even
Pound's worst political aberrations; a hatred of war (no
non-combatant has written more movingly of the sheer
waste of young life and talent which the First World
War involved); a hatred of the arms traffic, of a society
moved more and more by purely commercial motives,
the lust for money and power; of the kind of attitudes,
partly the gambler's, partly the prudent and conservative
banker's, the combined rashness and meanness of a free-for-
all economy, which lay perhaps partly behind the great
American slump of 1929 and the widespread unemploy-
ment of the 1930's. What Pound is often most fundamentally preaching in the *Cantos* is not Fascism or anti-Semitism
but the need for a corporate sense of social responsibility.

But, of course, there is a very real sense, which again should not be dodged, in which Pound *is* a "reactionary." To be "progressive" in our time is to wish both to raise the conditions of labour, of the labouring masses, and at the same time to approximate the conditions of life and of work of all those who are *not* labourers (for instance, priests, politicians, poets) to the conditions of labour; to be "progressive" is to dislike both natural hierarchies and functional, which is to say natural, privileges.

A very good clue, it seems to me, to Pound's general attitudes to society is to be found in Hannah Arendt's recent book, *The Human Condition*. Miss Arendt in this book makes a distinction between four levels of human functioning: labour, making, activity, contemplation. There is a sense in which making (craftsmanship, artistry) and activity (the function, say, of the statesman, the soldier, the explorer) and contemplation (the function of the saint, of the philosopher, and perhaps also, at a level beyond mere artistry, of the poet) all depend utterly on labour. Labour must always be the condition of the broad mass of men; and yet, for Miss Arendt, until he rises above the labouring condition, man is not fully human. In daily labour, the labouring man exhausts himself, and temporarily renews himself and us; he provides himself and us with, say, coal, bread, transport, milk, heat, light, water. Man as *animal laborans* produces no permanent memorial of himself; he produces what he, and we, daily consume in order to keep ourselves alive; daily, he exhausts himself, renews himself, dies and is reborn, according to the natural rhythms of life. He is very close to these. He is very close to these, but he works, Miss Arendt thinks, because he must eat, not for the work's sake; often he likes monotonous work that lets him daydream. And though he works in large groups, he is lonely; his work, essentially repetitive, does not involve complicated communication.

Man the artist or craftsman, on the other hand, *homo*

faber, strives to create a setting for his own individual life more permanent than that is, to transcend, in some way, labour's daily rhythm of exhaustion and renewal. It is *homo faber* who, with the help of labour, creates our "world"; our houses, our furniture, our cities, our art-works, everything that outlasts us and gives labour a point and a setting. His work, too, of course decays or is consumed in the end, like bread or milk, but not so rapidly. Men who pursue the still higher *vita activa* strive to create, not a world of permanent objects like poems or buildings, but the human story. They make speeches, fight battles, preach sermons, change men's minds. The highest level of all, for Miss Arendt, is the *vita contemplativa* in which man, often in solitude, seeks to confront and grapple with the ultimate meaning of things, God or the absence of God, the presence or absence of value in the human will or in the nature of things, what the human city is for, life's futility or its significance.

Pound, both as a poet and as a thinker, reveres the condition of labour, in so far as that has accumulated round it traditional skills invented by *homo faber*; but the heroes to whom he draws our attention in the *Cantos* are, on the whole, neither labouring men nor artists but representatives of the *vita activa* (Odysseus, Sigismundo de Malatesta, Thomas Jefferson, John Adams) or of the *vita contemplativa* directed to the nature of the human city (Confucius). He agrees with Miss Arendt (he disagrees with Carlyle) in not exalting the condition of labour in itself. We do not need, he thinks (and I think he is right), to toil at some monotonous task eight or ten hours a day in order to be good and happy. Labour is a necessary evil, or the sweat of it is. This feeling explains both his anti-Socialism and his interest in various Social Credit schemes. His theoretical economics may be extremely vulnerable; but his ideal of the good life as involving more leisure, more abundance, more individual freedom of choice, may be Utopian but it is not cranky. It is an artist's wishing for others what he wishes for himself; and it is, of course, the social groups who enjoy (perhaps unjustly) a margin of freedom and leisure who have always fostered art.

Yet this social ideal, which has so much, at least in abstraction, to be said for it, led Pound to a virulent intermittent anti-Semitism (of course, he has good Jewish friends, as many anti-Semites have), and to broadcasting, during the Second World War, from Italy, when the United States, at war with Italy, was helping to liberate Europe from an obscene tyranny. Here too Miss Arendt has, I think, if not an excuse, at least an explanation. She makes a very interesting distinction between three possible notes of an individual will, and of the civil society: violence, strength, and power. Violence, for her, is the mark of tyranny; it cuts off free communication between men; thus it makes the true *vita activa*, the life of practically persuasive public communication, impossible, though, strangely, *homo faber* flourishes under it (as he did in the Italian Renaissance). The naturally strong man can protect himself against tyrannical violence by stoical endurance or passive withdrawal. The strong man, however, who can protect himself against the violence of an individual tyrant, cannot protect himself against legally and constitutionally organised social power.

The will to organised power Miss Arendt sees as the mark, not of the strong, but of the weak, perhaps particularly of those bound to the condition of labour. She classes the will to power with greed and envy as a special characteristic of the weak; bending together, they can control the strong. In the society of job-holders, which Miss Arendt gloomily envisages as our future society, the poet, the statesman, the mystic will all be reduced to the status of wage-earners, of functionaries; what they produce will become, like the products of labour, essentially a set of daily necessities, rapidly perishable consumer's goods: one thinks of religious broadcasts, television plays, election speeches, this year's "new" novelist or playwright. Nothing will be done or made or thought to be memorable or last. Rapid usability, perishability will become an essential prerequisite of thought, art, action. I hope she is much too gloomy; but she is plausible; and these sentences of hers, for instance, give me a complete picture of the motives behind Pound's politics:

> If tyranny can be described as the always abortive attempt to substitute violence for power, ochlocracy, or mob rule, which is its exact counterpart, can be characterised by the much more promising attempt to substitute power for strength. Power indeed can ruin all strength, and we know that where the main public realm is society, there is always the danger that, through a perverted form of "acting together"—by pull and pressure and the tricks of cliques—those are brought to the fore who know nothing and can do nothing. The vehement yearning for violence, so characteristic of some of the best modern creative artists, thinkers, scholars, and craftsmen, is a natural reaction of those whom society has tried to cheat of their strength.[1]

That fits Pound like a glove. And there is another splendid paragraph of Miss Arendt's which seems to me to sum up, perhaps more briefly and cogently than he has ever done himself, Pound's insistence that we must "make it new," that the continuing health of any civilisation, of any civilisation particularly that cares for its roots, must depend on a daily effort of renewal, on the deliberate effort to turn habit into freshness of skill, accepted process into the sense that we are making, or remaking, history:

> Without action to bring into the play of the world the new beginning of which each man is capable by virtue of

being born, "there is no new thing under the sun ";
without speech to materialize and memorialize, however tentatively, the "new things" that appear and shine
"there is no remembrance"; without the enduring
permanence of a human artifact, there cannot "be any
remembrance of things that are to come with those
that shall come after." And without power, the space
of appearance brought forth through action and
speech in public will fade away as rapidly as the living
deed and the living word.[2]

The central intuition expressed there, so beautifully, is
Pound's central intuition, certainly in the *Cantos* quite
explicitly, but perhaps implicitly from his very earliest
poems onwards: the human need for the permanence of
the human artifact, the memorial, so that there shall con-
tinue to be "remembrance of things that are to come
with those that shall come after." There is in the passage
too his central sense of human action having to become
story, and story having to become lesson, if human life
is not to be reduced to the state of mere natural process.
And the last sentence suggests his great error in the *vita
activa*. He mistook the violence of Fascist dictatorship for
power, for something to build on; it was not. And seeing
many of the faults and failings of English and American
democracy throughout his lifetime he mistook that either
for ochlocracy, mob rule, the weak conspiring against the
strong, greed and envy conspiring against creative talent,
or for a thin mask of ochlocracy only half-concealing the
rule, a soulless rule, of money. Again, he was wrong.
But, wrong in his political hatreds, wrong in his political
enthusiasms, was he wrong in his central intuition of the
importance of tradition for culture?
I have thought it best to reverse the usual order of
biographical procedure, and to bring up the great moral
questions involved in Pound's story, before telling, very
briefly, that story itself. Having seen what the great

questions are, the reader, whether previously biased for or
against Pound, can now throw upon the story the dry
light of the mind.

Ezra Pound was born in 1885, in Hailey, Idaho, in the
Middle West of the United States. He passed through
Hamilton College and the state university of Pennsyl-
vania, took a Master's degree there in Romance Languages, and in 1907 was appointed lecturer in French
and Spanish at Wabash College, Crawfordsville, not
then one of the major American institutions of higher
learning. The appointment lasted for a very short time.
Pound was dismissed according to one account for being
"too much of a Latin quarter type." He showed, I have
been told, an innocent protective interest in a chorus girl
or ballet dancer stranded in Crawfordsville down on her
luck, and this the authorities, staunch Baptists or Pres-
byterians, did not like. Perhaps we can trace to this
episode Pound's lasting dislike and distrust of the con-
ventional academic mind and his belief that Protestant
Christianity is, almost of necessity, the enemy of happiness
and culture.

He decided, for the time being, to quit the States. He
made his way adventurously to Europe on a cattle-ship,
landed at Gibraltar, where he visited a synagogue and
made friends with local Jews (like many literary men
who can be charged with anti-Semitism, including for
instance Belloc who had a devoted Jewish secretary, and
Léon Daudet who was one of the closest friends and
warmest admirers of the half-Jew, Marcel Proust, Pound
has had many close friends among Jews). He walked
through Spain and Southern France to Venice. He had
his first book of poems published there under the title of
A Lume Spento (an English version might be "When the
Light Fades"). This came out, a small private edition,
in 1908. Later in the same year, Pound came to England,
where he was to remain till 1921.

In England, he lived mainly in London, settling finally

in a small flat near the foot of Kensington Church Street. He paid some visits to the Home Counties and, according to the *Cantos*, was as far west once as Salisbury Plain; but I cannot make out that he ever visited the Midlands, the North, Scotland, Ireland, or Wales. In one sense, he acquired a very intimate knowledge of England, but his main observation post was London, and especially literary London, literary London bohemian and experimental rather than established and fashionable. There is a sense in which, in his thirteen years in England, Pound, though he became very well known and was able to give a great deal of practical help to writers like Joyce and the young T. S. Eliot, never quite "arrived." His status, on his departure as on his arrival, was that of an interesting but disturbing and unpredictable "wild man." On his arrival, his red beard, his huge shock of blonde hair, his strong Mid-Western accent, and a general *naïveté*, eagerness, and desire to startle and impress made him an immediately notable figure, but not always a popular one. He stirred things up too much. Yet though he never, during his years in England, became a poet whom the general public "knew about," as they knew, say, about Masefield, Yeats, Bridges, Hardy, Rupert Brooke, and the Georgians and the poets of the First World War, his influence on new moods and new techniques in English verse was to be a profoundly important one.

Three short books of poems by Pound came out in 1909. In 1910, there was another book of poems, and also Pound's first prose book, *The Spirit of Romance*. He used the word "romance" in the title as it is used in the phrase "Romance Languages," and the book had a wide sweep from Silver Latin poets to Lope de Vega. It was praised by contemporary critics for its enthusiasm and faulted for blunders in translation and inaccuracy in quoting from, or using in English phrases from, foreign languages. It reflected two interests that became permanent in Pound's subsequent work; one was a sense of the Euro-

pean literary tradition, or the Mediterranean, Hellenis-
tic-Latin-Romance part of it, as a single whole: the other
was a passion for translation, for attempting to bring
over as vividly as possible into English effects of phrasing,
rhythm, cadence that had impressed Pound in foreign or
ancient tongues.

It is generally admitted today, I think, even by Pound's
warmest admirers, that this passion was not accompanied
by a scholarly scrupulousness about conveying the exact
prose sense of the poems he was translating; he was less
interested in sense than in what Dr I. A. Richards calls
tone and feeling, less interested in what he himself calls
logopoeia (the play of ideas in a poem, the imitation of discourse) than in what he calls *melopoeia* and *phanopoeia*
(roughly, music and images). In spite of some translations from Heine, and a great interest in the German
anthropologist Frobenius, and a brilliant if wildly inaccurate translation of the Anglo-Saxon *Seafarer*, Pound
never took up Teutonic languages with the same enthusiasm as Romance languages. He has never shown any
interest in Slavonic prose or poetry. He may have derived
his special interest in Villon and Cavalcanti from Rossetti
and Swinburne. They were a traditional Pre-Raphaelite
interest, as were the Troubadours; the father of one of
Pound's closest English friends, Ford Madox Hueffer
(later Ford Madox Ford), had written a little book about
the Troubadours, which may have quickened an interest
already aroused by Pound's university studies and his
wanderings in the south of France. At the end of the first
decade of the century, in the age of high journalism, the
age of Wells and Shaw and Chesterton and Belloc, the
age also of Kipling, these literary interests of the young
American visitor must have seemed rather touchingly
old-fashioned; a survival not merely from the 1890's, but
from the 1870's and the 1880's. The man who was to
become the greatest innovator, technically, in verse of
his time started off looking a picturesque back-number.

Pound's friends in London around 1910 included the philosopher-poet T. E. Hulme, later killed in the First World War, and the poet F. S. Flint. Both of these had an interest, which Pound was soon to share, in the Japanese *haiku* and *tanka*, the short traditional 17-syllable and 31-syllable poems which they knew mainly, I imagine (Japanese is a very difficult language indeed) through French translations. *Haiku* and *tanka* are extremely concise, allusive, and elliptical; they present, they do not comment; they work by images, not concepts; they imply a mood or a complex of feelings, they do not state it. They were at the root of what was to become Imagism, a theory of poetry as presentation divorced from commentary, and not tied down to an imposed metrical form. Also behind Imagism was a growing impatience felt by young poets with the staleness and conventionality of the diction and metre and sentiments of post-Victorian verse. Imagism, like nearly all the movements with which Pound has been associated during his long life, was a movement towards renewal and concentration of language. F. S. Flint has possibly more claims to be the originator of Imagism than Pound; but Pound with H. D. (Hilda Doolittle) and Richard Aldington was one of the leading lights of the movement, and the great spokesman and pusher of it; later, in the United States, Imagism was taken up by Amy Lowell, whose cruder or more diluted version of the theory Pound described rudely as Amygism. Pound's own Imagism is most to the fore in the selection of his poems called *Lustra*; there, however, he often blends the technique of the Japanese *haiku* with that of the Greek or Latin epigram. An anthology, *Des Imagistes*, anonymously edited by Pound, came out in 1914.

By 1914, however, in his own work, Pound had already left pure Imagism behind. He was widely extending the range of his interests, particularly in the fields of music, painting, and sculpture. He was a close friend of the brilliant sculptor Henri Gaudier-Brzeska, and of Percy

Wyndham Lewis, the founder of the English Vorticist
movement; he contributed to Lewis's explosive periodical
of violent dissent, *Blast*. But it is hard at any period of his
history to pin this multifarious man down to one set of
interests. Around 1912, he became a close friend of Yeats's,
taught him fencing, and introduced him to the newer
generation of English poets. Yeats noted Pound's
"rugged and headstrong nature," his capacity for
"hurting people's feelings," but also praised his good will
and was grateful to Pound for turning his mind away from
abstractions towards "the definite and concrete."

Pound spent the winter of 1912 to 1913 with Yeats in a
cottage at Holman's Hatch, acting as a kind of unofficial
secretary-companion. About this time, also, Pound was
working on the notes left behind him by the great American expert on Japanese art, Ernest Fenollosa. In their
basic structure and vocabulary, Chinese and Japanese
are languages quite unrelated to each other. Japanese,
however, is written in Chinese characters or ideograms,
with the addition of a syllabary: a character or ideogram
has primarily a semantic rather than a phonetic meaning. Chinese who speak quite different dialects can com-
municate to each other in writing; it is as if Westerners
had an ideogram which could indifferently be pronounced
"*chien*" and "dog." In addition, the Japanese have borrowed many concepts from China and in some cases have
adapted to Japanese pronunciation the original Chinese
pronunciation of a word (as English has borrowed many
concepts and basic phonetic patterns to go with them,
from Latin, but has altered these patterns to suit the
genius of the English language). Thus the name "Li-Po"
becomes in Japanese "Rihaku." Because of this complicated relationship between Japanese and Chinese, it is
possible for a good Japanese scholar to sight-translate a
classical Chinese poem into Japanese, without being able
to *speak* (in a sense, he is able to *read*) classical Chinese.

This was what Fenollosa had done with a number of

classical Chinese poems. He had then translated his
Japanese sight-readings into English prose. Fenollosa's
widow had come across Pound's poems, and been struck
by them. She sent Pound Fenollosa's prose Chinese-
through-Japanese translations, and his prose versions of
and notes on, Japanese Noh plays. Pound also edited, and
wrote an introduction to, Fenollosa's essay on *The
Chinese Written Character*. Chinese characters, which represent words or concepts, have now to be learned by young
Chinese or Japanese schoolboys as we learn the alphabet.
But originally some of them at least were sketchy picto-
grams, which conveyed an abstract idea by juxtaposing
two concrete images. Thus I have been told by a New
Zealand philosopher that the Chinese character for
"Peace" represents a house (the top of a triangle, representing a house) with *one* woman (three lines, with a
triangle going down from the waist, representing a skirt,
inside it); the Chinese character for "Strife" is the same
top-of-triangle house pictogram with *two* women inside
it. The Chinese character for the idea "Sunset" is similarly
a sketchily simplified version of a tree with a similarly
sketchy version of the sun under a high branch (I do not
see why this should not be *also* the Chinese character for
"Sunrise").

Complicated characters in Chinese are made by combining simple characters, each representing in a sense a
"particular," an image, and therefore Fenollosa thought,
and Pound agreed with him, Chinese thought can never
lose itself in vague abstraction. An abstract idea will
never, in Chinese, divorce itself from particular *exempla*;
it is as if, using the English language, we could never use
the word "justice" without visualising, at least in a rudi-
mentary fashion, a pair of scales, or the word "reverence" or "piety" without visualising, say, a son bowing to
a father. Pound, with his hatred of abstraction, pounced
on this. It is at the basis of the "ideogrammatic" manner
of procedure—many vivid examples, as few general state-

ments as possible—of the *Cantos*. Pound did his greatest
set of versions from the Chinese, *Cathay*, when he had
grasped this seminal idea, and did not know a word of
Chinese or Japanese. His later versions of the canonical
odes, the odes as established by the Confucians, though
written after thirty years' or so study of Chinese, strike
me as uninteresting compared with *Cathay*. This is partly,
of course, because Pound's interest has shifted, between
the later and earlier translations, from poems expressing
direct human feeling to celebratory poems, almost like
hymns, celebrating custom and ritual; I find this aspect
of Confucianism infinitely boring. But it is not only that.

The translations in *Cathay*, done with no real scholarly
equipment at all, have something that the scholarly *and*
poetical versions of Arthur Waley have not; the later
versions, done after thirty years' or so of amateurish
mugging up of Chinese, strike me as infinitely inferior, as
English poetry, to Waley. There is a queer sense in which
the more Pound "knows" about a subject, the less you
can rely on him; and *vice versa*. The essay on Guido
Cavalcanti is almost totally useless to an intelligent
amateur trying to work out what, in *Donna mi Prega*,
Cavalcanti really says; but a stray remark about Cavalcanti's rhythms seems impeccable. Pound, in fact, in his
incursions into learning, is like a brilliant but unmethodi-
cal schoolboy. He has an opening insight, an intuition of
what the subject is going to be like, of what the heart of
it is, that is wonderful; but little patience for homework.
A hatred for "abstraction" after all implies a hatred for
certain established Western processes of learning. Mug
up your irregular verbs, do your dull proses, before you
attempt to appreciate poetry in a foreign language. A
good teacher always tells his pupils that a subject must
be dull, there must be a great deal of grind in it, before it
becomes interesting. A poet like Pound wants it to be
interesting at once, short-circuits, short-cuts; sometimes
successfully, but sometimes blowing a fuse, sometimes

skidding off the road. It is always dangerous, in the long run, to attempt to dispense entirely with grind, or, which is similar though not the same thing, to do it all by yourself, instead of putting yourself under masters, who may be bores, but have mastered the subject.

The last two or three paragraphs may seem a rather lengthy digression in a mainly biographical chapter, but it is also a chapter about ideological background, context, climate of ideas. Without the impact of Fenollosa on Pound, we would not have the "ideogrammatic" method of the *Cantos*: the juxtaposition of scenes, images, episodes (like the juxtaposition of simple Chinese characters in a complex Chinese character, branch and sun under it meaning sunset) to spark off an abstract idea. Without the wish to go for the essence, the important thing, first of all, and without the impatience with all kinds of heavy-footed point-by-point donnish procedures, we would not have the inaccuracies of some of Pound's translations or the wilfulness of some of his opinions. It is odd, for instance, to take your economics from Douglas and Gessell without having made some previous attempt to master, say, Adam Smith, Ricardo, Marx, Marshall.

The tendency to short-circuit, to short-cut means that Pound sometimes gives an authority, both in his general prose writing and in his poetry, to people, books, ideas whose main source of authority is that, at some period in his life, they happen dramatically to have impinged on him. A man is interesting because Pound knew him; a poem because Pound took the trouble to read it; an idea because Pound has mulled over it.

I think this may be behind one of Pound's favourite words about ethics and economics, in his prose works, "volitional." I only know the word elsewhere in theological contexts, where volitionalism is the theory that what God wills is good because He wills it; the opposite to this theory is rationalism, the theory that God wills what is good because it is good. Volitionalism has obviously a

good deal in common with William James's pragmatism;
the typically American theory that a belief or a set of
attitudes that "works" for us up to a point is so far "true."
I am a rationalist, not a volitionalist, or a pragmatist. I
do not think my willing (or God's willing for that matter)
can make the intrinsic nature of a moral situation other
than what it is; God can forgive me for a bad act; He
cannot make it a good act. And, rather similarly, if I lose
a game, it is, on the whole, because I have played it
badly. There may be another sense of "volitionalism,"
that we need a high discipline of the will to preserve, to
defend, to bring into being good states of affairs, and in
this sense it may be defensible.

What Pound believes, however, and it comes out in
some of his greatest poetry, is that it is the intensity of
willing which creates the good, perhaps creates the real:
but willing with this degree of intensity should be called
love. The key passage for the deepest understanding of
his profoundest philosophy, religion, or whatever else it
should be called, is perhaps this from the *Pisan Cantos*:

> What thou lovest well remains,
> > the rest is dross
> What thou lov'st well shall not be reft from thee
> What thou lov'st well is thy true heritage
> Whose world, or mine or theirs
> > or is it of none?
> First came the seen, then thus the palpable
> > Elysium, though it were in the halls of hell,
> What thou lovest well is thy true heritage
> What thou lov'st well shall not be reft from thee[3]

There is an undeniable nobility there; and one way of
understanding Pound is by seeing him as a man who, in
a world which has been for him often enough, personally,
and in its general drift and shape, "the halls of hell," has
willed and loved intensely enough to create passages of
poetry, concentrations of vision, that are for the time

being "the palpable Elysium." Hell, it should be noted, is not for Pound quite a Christian hell; you do not get through it, or out of it, he tells "the Reverend Mr Eliot," in a hurry; but you might get out of it some time.

It was in 1915 that Pound first met the young Eliot, then not at all a clerical or sermonical young man. He compiled a miscellany of poems, *Catholic Anthology*— catholic in the sense of eclectic, ranging, universal, not in the sense of Roman Catholic—with the purpose of getting "sixteen pages of Eliot into print at once." The sixteen pages included "Prufrock" and "Portrait of a Lady," almost undergraduate poems, which Conrad Aiken had handled for Eliot, without managing to interest any magazine or publisher, since about 1913. Around the same period, Pound got the Egoist Press to publish James Joyce's *Portrait of the Artist as a Young Man*, and arranged for instalments of *Ulysses* to appear in *The Little Review* in America; and he persuaded Miss Harriet Weaver to give Joyce enough money to finish *Ulysses* in comfort. He was also encouraging the brilliant young sculptor, Henri Gaudier-Brzeska. His extraordinary gift for discovering and helping geniuses did not, however, at all, help towards any sort of recognised central position in London letters. Two long poems written between the outbreak of the Great War and its immediate aftermath, *Hugh Selwyn Mauberley* and "Homage to Sextus Propertius," reflect Pound's disgust at the commercialisation and cheapening of culture, his hatred of brassy jingoistic literature, his sense of the waste of the Great War; that war carried off two close friends, Gaudier-Brzeska and T. E. Hulme; two other friends, Wyndham Lewis and Ford Madox Ford, saw service.

Pound had married, in 1914, Dorothy Shakespear, the daughter of a London solicitor and of Yeats's close friend of the 1890's, Olivia Shakespear. He has a son, whom I have met, and a daughter, in whose husband's castle in the Italian Tyrol he is now living. Perhaps the growing responsibilities of family life, and the difficulty of getting an established literary position in London, made him feel the need of a move; perhaps he felt he had exhausted England; certainly the English post-war scene depressed him. I have been told that he was done out of an assistant editorship on the *Athenaeum*, on which he had relied for five pounds a week or so, by Middleton Murry. At any rate, in 1921 he settled in Paris, where he lived till 1925. He made new friends there, Gertrude Stein, Brancusi, Jean Cocteau, the young Ernest Hemingway. He wrote a book about a musical protegé, the young Polish-American composer, George Antheil. He wrote also the libretto and music of an opera about Villon (it has been performed on the B.B.C.). He began to pursue an interest in economics, which had its roots in a meeting with Major C. H. Douglas, of the Douglas Credit scheme, in 1917. This interest plays a large and to many readers a puzzling part in the *Cantos*: but Pound's hatred of usury, or his distrust of finance capitalism, or of a completely "free" economy, is not so eccentric as some critics have made out. Distrust of the power of banks is traditional in American politics since Andrew Jackson, so is the wish, felt especially by farmers and pioneer entre-preneurs, for cheap money. And economic ideas with at least a family resemblance to Pound's can be found, for instance, in Cobbett, Carlyle, Ruskin, and R. H. Tawney.

In 1925 (perhaps he was getting a little tired of the constant stream of young American geniuses arriving in Paris) Pound moved to the Italian coastal resort of Rapallo, where he had Max Beerbohm (they played tennis together, and gently mocked each other) as a distinguished neighbour. He admired the early achieve-ments of Fascism which was, at that time, neither a racialist nor a militantly imperialist movement. The study of Italian history helped to feed new material into the *Cantos*, which were now becoming his main preoccupation. In 1938, he visited America for the first time in over twenty years, and received an honorary degree at his old university. Two years earlier he had published *Jefferson and/or Mussolini*, a book suggesting, not very plausibly and very tactlessly at that particular juncture, that Mussolini and the better American Founding Fathers, for all the difference of abstract principles, stood for a broadly similar attitude to the problem of efficiently governing a country. Throughout the 1930's, Pound's sympathy with Mussolini had made him growingly disliked and distrusted in "progressive" circles both in Great Britain and the United States.

This feeling was so strong that when, on the outbreak of war between America and the Axis powers, Pound tried to get back to America, he was prevented from doing so, even though he and his wife had already booked their air passage. When, in 1942, he tried to join the diplomatic train taking Americans from Italy to Lisbon, permission was again refused. The basis of both refusals was probably broadcasts that Pound had been making from Rome Radio, quite legally but certainly exceedingly imprudently, before America's entry into the Second World War; he can have had no conception of the depth of American detestation of the Axis and sympathy with the Allied cause, even before Pearl Harbor. Eight weeks after America's entry into the war, Pound asked the Italian Ministry of Popular Culture for permission to resume these broadcasts, with the condition that he should not be subject to directives or censorship. These broadcasts led to his arrest by the American Army, after interrogation, in 1945. He had been indicted for treason, in his absence, by the Grand Jury of the District Court of Columbia in 1943. The indictment ran to thirteen counts. He remonstrated against it through Switzerland. This indictment was superseded, after his arrest, by another in October 1945.

After being interrogated at Genoa by the American

Army, Pound was taken by road to Pisa, where he was put in solitary confinement in a barbed wire cage. There was no roof, but he had three blankets. Nobody was allowed to speak to him, and searchlights were trained on him at night. This kept him from sleeping. After six weeks of this treatment, he had a severe nervous breakdown, and was removed to the greater comfort of a tent. He had two books with him, a Confucius in Chinese, and a Bible. Some kind negro soldiers provided him with a table of sorts, and writing materials. Recovering from his breakdown, he composed the first draft of the *Pisan Cantos*, in which the landscape round the camp plays an important part, and translated two Confucian texts.

In November 1945, Pound was flown to Washington to be tried, on the indictment drawn up in the previous month, for treason. On the eve of his trial, he was submitted to medical examination, and was declared unfit to plead. The Medical Board's report deserves, as a kind of document which is rarely available in the history of a great poet, to be quoted in full:

The defendant, now sixty years of age and in generally good physical condition, was a precocious student, specialising in literature. He has been a voluntary expatriate for nearly forty years, living in England and France and for the past twenty-one years in Italy, making an uncertain living by writing poetry and criticism. His poetry and literary criticism have received considerable recognition, but in recent years his pre-occupation with monetary theory and economics has apparently obstructed his literary productivity. He has long been recognized as eccentric, querulous, and ego-centric. At the present time, he exhibits extremely poor judgment as to his situation. He insists that his broadcasts were not treasonable but that all of his radio activities have stemmed from his self-appointed mission to 'save the Constitution.' He is abnormally grandiose, is expansive and exuberant in manner, exhibiting pressure of speech, discursiveness, and distractability.

In our opinion, with advancing years his personality, for many years abnormal, has undergone further distortion to the extent that he is now suffering from a paranoid state which renders him mentally unfit to advise properly with counsel or to participate reasonably and intelligently in his own defence. He is, in other words, insane and mentally unfit for trial, and in need of care in a mental hospital.[4]

I think that is an admirably humane document, in its expression a model of professional lucidity without jargon. And I am very glad, for Pound's sake, that the Medical Board arrived at this decision; if he had been put on trial, it would have been impossible to acquit and politically very difficult to pardon him. I have seen transcripts only of a very few of his broadcasts, mainly on literary subjects; I have been told that others contained virulently anti-Semitic propaganda. Pound no doubt thought very sincerely that, in giving them, he was defending America, or what America should be. But, of course, whatever the content had been, making the broadcasts at all laid him open to an indictment for treason; America was at war with Italy, he was, by broadcasting from an Italian station, giving aid and comfort to the enemy, and that was that. The decision of the Medical Board saved him from life imprisonment, perhaps from death.

At the same time, some of the remarks in the report make me wonder just how sane, by the verdict of a committee of psychiatrists, any poet is. I have known a great many poets in my time. A great majority of them "make an uncertain living by writing poetry and criticism"; good poets often do tend to be "grandiose, expansive and exuberant in manner"; they can also often be recognised (especially when one of their books has been reviewed unfavourably, or a rival poet is getting too much publicity) as "eccentric, querulous, and egocentric." They quite often do have some obsessional interest, that seems at first sight to have little to do with poetry, like Pound's economics. Perhaps all poets *are* a little mad; one talks of "mad poets" as one talks of "mad majors." The creative process puts a continuing strain on the whole organism, on the intelligence and sensibility, and in a way also it isolates the creative person, in a way that the uncreative (however full of intelligence and good will) may find it hard to understand.

Pound was sent to St Elizabeth's Hospital, a large public mental hospital in the suburbs of Washington. He spent fifteen months in a large concrete dormitory without furniture or windows, in which every second occupant was confined in a sort of straitjacket. He was then moved to a smaller room with eight or nine beds, and then, after eighteen months was given a tiny cubicle, a table, a typewriter, the opportunity to write and receive visitors regularly. His period in hospital was, in fact, a very productive one. He translated a play of Sophocles and the whole of the canonical Chinese *Book of Odes* and kept on working at the *Cantos*; he also kept up a large correspondence with friends.

Some English friends of my own, John Wain, Denis Goacher, Alfred Alvarez, all visited Pound at St Elizabeth's. They all felt very sorry for him, and found his personality gentle and endearing. But some of them thought that Pound had taken a battering from life that had left him, in a sense, permanently mentally unstable. One asked some question about Yeats, and Pound replied: "I can't answer that, the top of my head's not working." Since writing this, I have found almost the same story in Stephen Splender's *World within World*. This was perhaps Pound's routine answer to questions about Yeats. (It is possible to see this, however, as a typically Poundian joke.) In both the United States and

Great Britain committees of sympathisers from the very beginning of Pound's confinement in St Elizabeth's were agitating, or thinking out means to agitate, for his release. In 1947, the *Washington Post* reported the American Government as refusing to release Pound to the custody of his family on the grounds that "transfer to a private institution would merely place him in a happier and more comfortable position"; but, if he was thought genuinely insane, and not responsible for his actions, why not? One also heard it sometimes urged that if Pound were, as it were, "declared sane," he would still be liable for trial on his indictment; so might it not be more humane, on the balance, to leave him where he was?

In 1949, Pound received the Bollingen Award, a prize of 1000 dollars, for the *Pisan Cantos*, which had just been published as a separate volume (they are now in the collected *Cantos*). This award raised a tremendous controversy, though the very distinguished panel of judges included T. S. Eliot, Robert Lowell, W. H. Auden, and Conrad Aiken. The crux of the debate was something like this; poetry expressing evil opinions (anti-Semitism, sympathy with Fascism) cannot really be great or good poetry; or, on the other hand, if it *is* great or good poetry in spite of expressing evil opinions, then the moral status, the public usefulness, of poetry itself is called very sharply into question. *Partisan Review*, a magazine standing in politics for the opposite of everything Pound stands for, and with a largely Jewish editorial board, to its great credit published a lively and generous symposium, not weighted either way, on the award and also a fine article by John Berryman on Pound's art in verse.

A year or two ago, in a milder climate of opinion, Pound was released from St Elizabeth's, and went to Italy, to join his daughter in her husband's castle in the Tyrol. He gave interviews to the B.B.C. and for television on his release, and made B.B.C. recordings, with a commentary, on some of the *Cantos*; he has more recently given three rich and various interviews, on all aspects of his life, to D. G. Bridson, a feature producer on the B.B.C.'s Third Programme. And he goes on adding to the *Cantos*; the latest instalment of these, *Thrones*, has come out, in fact, just as I have been putting the finishing touches to this book, too late for me to include a critical consideration of it.

I speak elsewhere in this book of the touch of the actor or preacher which I detected in these recent broadcasts of Pound's. More fundamental than that perhaps is a kind of serenity and unhurtness, a resilience and a cheerfulness extraordinary when one considers all he has gone through, all the violence of his opinions, all the violence with which the world has reacted against these. He repeated several times to Bridson the statement that what keeps a poet alive is curiosity; where curiosity dies, there technique becomes dull. His own curiosity is still alive. Never losing his lust for new languages, he is learning, with the help of his son-in-law, ancient Egyptian, and translating poems from that language. His mind is still busy with the problems of taxation and interest and credit. He is still full of enthusiasm for sacred books. The Common Law, as expounded by Coke or Blackstone, is, for him, something like the wisdom of Confucius; a support for order in the West. At the end of the last of Bridson's programmes, he read Uncle Remus's tarbaby story to his little grandson; so beautifully that, while one was laughing, one also wanted to cry.

It is very easy to moralise about a poet like Pound. America bred him; in England he became a man of letters. In England's hour of need, and America's, he seemed to be on the other side. I think it might be more profitable to turn the moralising the other way round. Here was this man with certainly an exceptional gift, in his own art, and for discovering and helping other artists. His own country sacked him from his first job. In Great Britain, he was never treated as much more than an amusing eccentric. It was not unnatural that he should deduce that a certain indifference, or even hostility, to art as such is a mark of liberal and democratic societies, of, in a broad sense, the Protestant tradition. So he went to Paris, and then to Italy, where the artist is a somebody; where he was a somebody; and it was natural that, in Italy, he should acquire a respect and a tolerance for the politics of a country which, at last, treated him with proper respect. The typical bureaucrat will deduce from the history of Pound the lesson that any notably original artist, especially an artist with an interest in the culture of other countries than his own, is a gross security risk. The genuine liberal (much as Pound dislikes liberals) will draw a sadder moral. How liberal is what we call a liberal culture? Where commercial values, and pressures for conformity, and the envies and fears of mediocrity prevail, how many of our poets and artists do we drive into exile, opposition, eccentricity, perhaps madness, perhaps treason? Are the artists, these unstable creatures, mainly to blame? Or are we, society at large, more to blame, for not treating them with the respect they deserve, giving them the honour that is their due, or even beginning to learn the lessons that we could learn from them? As long as we think of culture as a kind of extra, a luxury, a hobby, that we can indulge after we have used our best energies in the serious business of making money (or seeking power) cases like that of Ezra Pound are bound to recur. In a community where values were arranged more on the scale of their natural hierarchy—contemplation, action, making, labour—such tragedies would not happen.

REFERENCES

1. Hannah Arendt, *The Human Condition*, Doubleday Anchor Books, New York 1959, p. 182.

2. H. Arendt, *The Human Condition*, p. 183.

3. *The Cantos of Ezra Pound*, London 1954, p. 556.

4. From a pamphlet *Ezra Pound: Written on behalf of the Committee formed to Obtain his Release*, with a foreword by Richard Davies, privately printed, London 1956, p. 7.

CHAPTER II

THE WORK IN VERSE AND PROSE

I want in this chapter to give a chronological account of Pound's development as a poet, fairly abundantly illustrated by quotation, and by mainly technical comment on what I quote. I discussed Pound's ideas in my first chapter, and will discuss what some of his critics say about him in my next. I am not trying to judge the man or the poet in this chapter, but to act rather like a guide (I hope a reasonably well-informed and sensitive one) taking a party of reasonably intelligent visitors round an art gallery. This is what to look for; this leads on to this.

The reasons for writing a long and unwieldy chapter, like this, rather than breaking Pound up into "phases," are these. Pound has been writing poetry for more than fifty years, but it seems to me that since his early twenties, since he began writing, he has changed on the whole remarkably little as a person. He does not carve up easily, like Yeats, into early, middle, late, and latest; there is no central poem of spiritual crisis in his work, like Eliot's *Ash Wednesday*. He started in a pretty definite direction as a young poet, and has stuck to it, accumulating experience, refining technique, but never reaching a moment of crisis or revulsion, a sense that his compass or his world was broken, a need to find a new north. He must be a man of extraordinarily solid physical health and energy; he has kept the hardness of youth. On the other hand, as a craftsman, he has been developing continually, or facing bafflement continually, but not in a way that estranges his earlier work from his later.

Yeats in a sense almost completely remade his earlier

poems, to fit in with his later image of what his youth
should have been; Robert Graves is continually revising,
purifying his earlier poems to make them come up to his
present standards. These two fine poets changed, at
some stage, their idea of what a poet is, of what a poem
should be. Pound's ideal of what a poet is, and what
poetry is, remains, I would think, the ideal of his adoles-
cence; what he has done, over more than fifty years, is to
work harder and harder, in a growingly more large-
scale, complex, and ambitious way, to *realise* his youthful
ideal. So one must take him in a lump. I shall have a few
sketchy pages about his criticism at the end of this chapter; but the sort of thing he says, the sort of gesture he
makes, in his criticism is just the sort of thing or gesture
he says or makes in his poetry. He has an extraordinary
consistency or coherency, from the start to now: those
who like him will admire this; those who dislike him will
say, "Boloney is still boloney, cut it where you will."

Pound started as what he still is, fundamentally, a
"literary" poet rather than a "life" poet. Let us consider,
for instance, this very early poem, "Balatetta":

> The light became her grace and dwelt among
> Blind eyes and shadows that are formed as men:
> Lo, how the night doth melt us into song!
>
> The broken sunlight for a healm she beareth
> That hath my heart in jurisdiction.
> In wild-wood never fawn nor fallow fareth
> So silent light; no gossamer is spun
> So delicate as she is, when the sun
> Drives the clear emeralds from the bended grasses
> Lest they should parch too quickly, where she passes.[1]

The diction, there, even the pronunciation, is deliberately
archaic: the word "jurisdiction" has to be, as in Jacobean
poetic English, five, not four, syllables, "jurisdictíon."
The topic is a Renaissance commonplace, the beloved as

a goddess, specifically here Diana. The words are chosen for their literary associations, "wild-wood"; for a vivid preciosity (dew as "clear emeralds"); or for verbal texture, vowel and consonant harmony, like "fawn and fallow." There is no attempt at any sort of originality of feeling or matter; this is not a poem, like so many English contemporary poems of this decade (Philip Larkin's, for instance) shyly disguising the fact that it is "poetic," but the poem being "poetic" for all it is worth. The poem is a kind of "exercise." But what lifts it above mere respectful parody or sickly pastiche is the masterly sense of rhythm, the faultless ear.

I think this unerring sense of rhythm is Pound's basic gift. The quality of such an early poem is what Pound himself calls *melopoeia*, or music, melody-making. He developed his gift for *phanopoeia*, or vividness, realisation, image-making, later. He has never, I think, except perhaps in *Hugh Selwyn Mauberley*, become an absolute master of what he calls *logopoeia*, word-making or thought-making, the apt playing together of words and ideas (not of sound, or perception, but of concept) in poetry. This failure, I think, is largely due to the fact that for most of his creative life Pound has been an alien either to the language (as in Paris or Rapallo) or, as in London, to the idiom of the language current around him. This has made his own idiom very eccentric and individual; and has made him a talker rather than a listener.

Pound retained, during all his years in London, a strong late-nineteenth-century Idaho accent. D. G. Bridson's three brilliant interviews with Pound on the B.B.C.'s Third Programme have made many admirers of Pound rather disconcertedly familiar with Pound's spoken voice. When Pound reads poetry aloud, there is a kind of underdrone, a musical groaned base. There is an artificial elongation of long syllables, which often makes his verse sound quantitative, in the Greek or Latin manner. And there is a very strong emphasis, a resonance,

a reverberation, which sometimes suggests that Pound is
about to burst into song; sometimes, on the other hand,
that he is in the middle of a sermon or a political oration.
There is never an effect, or an imitation, of easy natural
speech.

I listened in to a repeat of these Third Programme
broadcasts of Pound's some time ago with a young
French friend. "*Un comédien?*" I asked her. Her reply was:
"*Pas un comédien, un tragédien. Il exagère.*" The English of
this little exchange would be: "An actor?"—"No, not an
actor, a ham—he overdoes it!" Certainly, Pound speaks
poetry aloud with "something above a mortal mouth";
the voice, with its elongation of vowels, its *miaulement*, the
full value which it gives to every syllable, its biting *r*s
(more biting than those of many Scotsmen or Ulster-
men) seems quite unlike most English voices, but strangely
unlike also one's current notion of an American voice.
It is, the young American poet Donald Hall said in a
Third Programme critical commentary on Pound's
broadcasts, "the *old* American voice." It is Idaho of the
1880's, say, still uncannily speaking to us.

Another notable (and to be continuing) thing in
Pound's earliest poems is the passion for translation.
Quoting fragments, I shall now give references. Let me
quote two examples from the poems before 1910, which
also illustrate the continuity of Pound's interests. One
is from Propertius, on whose work he was later to base
perhaps the greatest of his long-short poems, "Homage to
Sextus Propertius":

> Here let thy clemency, Persephone, hold firm,
> Do thou, Pluto, bring here no greater harshness.
> So many thousand beauties are gone down to Avernus,
> Ye might let one remain above with us.
> With you is Iope, with you the white gleaming Tyro,
> With you is Europa and the shameless Pasiphae,
> And all the fair from Troy and all from Achaia. . . .[2]

About Bertrans de Born, the troubadour who is in
Dante's Hell, the "stirrer up of strife," Pound was also to
write one of his greatest long-short poems, "Near Peri-
gord": he has a beautiful early translation of Bertrans's
Planh or lament for one of the troublesome sons of Henry
II, "the young English king":

> If all the grief and woe and bitterness,
> All dolour, ill and every evil chance
> That ever came upon this grieving world
> Were set together they would seem but light
> Against the death of the young English King.
> Worth lieth riven and Youth dolorous,
> The world o'ershadowed, soiled and overcast,
> Void of all joy and full of ire and sadness . . .[3]

These are versions, in both cases, of the expression (the
masterly expression) of a poetic commonplace. There is no
attempt to freshen that up by a modernised diction. The
words of the Propertius version ("many thousand
beauties," "all the fair") are those that would be appro-
priate in a Bohn or Loeb version in "timeless" English.
The *words* of the version from Bertrans de Born are the
common currency of pre-Raphaelite medievalism, the
medievalism of Swinburne and Rossetti ("evil chance,"
"riven," "dolorous," "full of ire"). What is remarkable
about these passages is their rhythmical resource, the
convincing way in which they bring over, in English unrhymed verse, as lyric and as elegy, an equivalent for the
rhythmical effect of their originals; it is worth noticing,
for instance, how the preponderance of unrhymed feminine endings to lines (endings not on a strong syllable)
reinforces the elegiac effect.

In the first translation, for instance, there are the endings, "harshness," "Avernus," "above with us," "Tyro,"
"Pasiphae," "Achaia"; in the second, against a clang of
strong endings, "bitterness," "dolourous," "sadness,"
and the endings on muted accents, "young English

Kìng," and "óvercàst." The preponderant influences of
Milton and Shakespeare had, throughout the nineteenth
century, made unrhymed verse growingly unusable; and
it was thought of preponderantly as a medium for dramatic, narrative, or ruminative verse; Pound has always
loathed Milton and has never been very enthusiastic
about Shakespeare. Approaching the possibilities of
unrhymed verse through the Latin elegiac couplet or
through the Provençal *planh* or sestina (where the same
words, or the same rhymes, recur not within the stanza
but within successive stanzas) he was able to renew unrhymed verse, for the English language, as a primarily
lyrical medium. This mastery of cadence is his great
early quality.

In the poems gathered in the collected volume as
Ripostes (1912) there are some early examples of the
imagist technique—worked out in more detail in the
succeeding group, *Lustra*—but more important perhaps is
the movement from metrically regular unrhymed verse
to free verse, and the more ambitious exercises in translation. There is a short poem in *Ripostes* which invites comparison with the already quoted Propertius version:

THE PICTURE

> The eyes of this dead lady speak to me,
> For here was love, not to be drowned out,
> And here desire, not to be kissed away.
> The eyes of this dead lady speak to me.[4]

Set against the Propertius version, this gains power by
expressing a broadly similar sentiment—lament and
yearning for dead beauty—by compression and simplicity, avoiding "direct" expression of the emotion. Notice
how the endings "drowned out" and "kissed away," with
the half-muted final accent, nicely, again, balance between a masculine and feminine ending. Or one can
compare with "Balatetta" this little poem on a similar
topic (the beloved as wood-nymph) in free verse:

A GIRL

The tree has entered my hands,
The sap has entered my arms,
The tree has grown in my breast—
Downward,
The branches grow out of me like arms.

Trees you are,
Moss you are,
You are violets with wind above them.
A child—so high—you are,
And all this is folly to the world.[5]

Set against "Balatetta," this gains freshness and directness (it is no longer a primarily "literary" poem) at the
cost of risking the appearance of *naïveté*. The great translation in *Ripostes* is that of the Anglo-Saxon *Seafarer*,
much attacked by scholars, but a very strong influence
for instance on Pound's own versions from the Chinese,
perhaps also on Waley's. One notices in it a more muscu-
lar, vigorous quality of language, a greater complexity
of feeling brought over, when one compares it with some
of the earlier translations:

        . . . Lest man know not
    That he on dry land loveliest liveth,
    List how I, care-wretched, on ice-cold sea,
    Weathered the winter, wretched outcast
    Deprived of my kinsmen;
    Hung with hard ice-flakes, where hail-scur flew,
    There I heard naught save the harsh sea
    And ice-cold wave, at whiles the swan cries,
    Did for my games the gannet's clamour,
    Sea-fowls' loudness was for me laughter,
    The mews' singing all my mead-drink.
    Storms, on the stone cliffs beaten, fell on the stern
    In icy feathers; full oft the eagle screamed
    With spray on his pinion. . . .[6]

It is interesting to compare the movement of these lines with the movement, for instance, of the opening of one of T. S. Eliot's most important early poems, "Gerontion":

> Here I am, an old man, in a dry month,
> Being read to by a boy, waiting for rain.
> I was neither at the hot gates
> Nor fought in the warm rain
> Nor knee deep in the salt marsh, heaving a cutlass,
> Bitten by flies, fought.[7]

"Gerontion" is one of Eliot's most accomplished earlier pieces of stylistic tesselation, and it soon modulates into other styles, notably pastiche of *The Revenger's Tragedy* and *The Changeling*. But that opening seems to come very much from Pound's adaptation of the old English line: and the peculiar glum wintry mood of "The Seafarer" seems to me also to be the underlying mood of "Gerontion." Pound's misunderstandings of the sense of his original are, in comparison with the power of "The Seafarer" as a new creation, unimportant; the late Gavin Bone's versions of old English poetry are free from such howlers; but, since Bone was not a poet, they will have no effect on contemporary English verse. "The Seafarer" seems to me to be one of Pound's greatest rehandlings; it helped him, because there the themes of exile, distance, wandering, the mood of nostalgic stoicism recur, in his marvellous rehandlings of Chinese classical poetry, the set of poems he calls *Cathay*.

The selection of poems called *Ripostes* is followed, in the English edition of Pound's collected shorter poems, by about forty pages of mainly very short poems called *Lustra*. These are the first batch of poems which, in the years preceding the First World War, the years between 1910 and 1914, when most of them seem to have been written, begin to make Pound look not like a belated Pre-Raphaelite, with a completely individual sense of rhythm, but like a consciously, even self-consciously,

"modernist" poet. There is an important change in the
diction. The diction of most, not quite all, of the poems up
to *Ripostes* is old world, and even olde-worlde; even
Wardour Street. People who dislike Pound and want to do
him down can, in the poems up to about 1910, find plenty
of stuff as embarrassing in its lingo as the historical novels
of Maurice Hewlett (Pound loved these, and was a great
chum of Hewlett's) or Stevenson's *Black Arrow*. Take this:

> Towards the Noel that morte saison
> (*Christ make the shepherds' homage dear!*)
> Then when the grey wolves everychone
> Drink of the winds their chill small-beer
> And lap o' the snows food's gueredon
> Then makyth my heart his yule-tide cheer
> (Skoal! with the dregs if the clear be gone!)
> Wining the ghosts of yester-year.[8]

When I was a boy in the late 1920's and early 1930's in
Aberdeen, a Scottish city characterised by a fierce reticence about the easy expression of human emotions, my
young sister and I used to go almost every Saturday after-
noon to the movies, the old silent pictures; during the
more excessively sentimental episodes of a movie my
sister would lower her eyes and begin, in sheer embarrassment, to chew the fingers of her cotton-gloves. This is
still a habit of hers when attending the theatre. We invented a family adjective based on this habit of hers, an
adjective to be applied to any kind of hamminess, any
kind of easy relapsing into stock responses, any cinema-
organ use of the *vox humana* stop, in human emotion or
art: the adjective glove-sucky. A number of Pound's early
poems are glove-sucky. "Villonaud for this Yule," which
I have just quoted, and its companion-piece, "A Villonaud: Ballad of the Gibbet" have the same grating effect
on me as the noise of the squeaking of chalk on a black-
board. And there is the shockingly embarrassing, the
extremely glove-sucky, "Ballad of the Goodly Fere,"

about Jesus, supposed to be the reminiscences of St Peter, shortly after the crucifixion:

> Aye he sent us out through the crossed high spears
> And the scorn of his laugh rang free,
> 'Why took ye me not when I walked about
> Alone in the town?' says he.
>
> Oh we drunk his 'Hale' in the good red wine
> When we last made company,
> No capon priest was the Goodly Fere
> But a man o' men was he. . . .
>
> They'll no' get him a' in a book I think
> Though they write it cunningly;
> No mouse of the scrolls was the Goodly Fere
> But aye loved the open sea.[9]

It tells one something about the solid power of human bad taste that this was one of the most popular, one of the most widely anthologised of Pound's early poems: Christ as Teddy Roosevelt, "alone in Cubia," the man with the big stick. But, like the "Villonauds," it is what might be called an *honest* bad poem (like "We are Seven," for instance): our embarrassment is not in any sense because Pound is faking up an emotion, but because this is the emotion that, heaven help us, he is uncritically accepting and expressing.

Lustra is an important set of poems, therefore, not merely technically but as marking a growth in sophistication (in the favourable sense of that ambiguous word) and of an ironically self-critical self-awareness. Pound's diction, or his sense of *logopoeia*, never became a conversational diction in the sense that the diction, say, of Pope in his verse epistles, of Byron in *Don Juan*, of Robert Frost, of Robert Graves, of Auden in many of his poems of the 1930's, of Philip Larkin today in England or Robert Lowell in his more recent American poems is conversational. A conversational diction is the product of highly

conscious art, but the art is directed towards making a
highly artificial and drastically concentrated construction sound like, have a resonance like, a man talking
naturally. It dramatises the natural: John Betjeman is
another contemporary master of it, and William Empson
also, when he is not being sardonically sublime. What lies
behind the high conversational tone in poetry is absolute
social assurance; one lives in one's set, has one's place in
one's set, and if one talks one will be listened to.

Pound never had that. He did not speak English in the
same way, in his London years, as the people around
him; had preoccupations and interests that they might
not share; was the observing alien, like Henry James, and,
like Henry James, as he develops his style towards sophistication he very oddly juxtaposes ironically formal,
mandarin language and a kind of slanginess around
which hover invisible inverted commas. The first paragraph of James's great novel *The Ambassadors*, is a classical
example of this consciously mandarin style besprinkled,
variegated, and made memorable by interspersions of
consciously demotic speech. Consciousness, or selfconsciousness, is what marks the mandarin-demotic
mode; it is the mode also of Eliot's earliest important
poems, "Prufrock" and "Portrait of a Lady." It owes
something in the nineteenth century to Laforgue and
Tristan Corbière in France, a great deal to Browning in
England. It is the tone not of unselfconscious assurance,
like the true conversational style, but of very intelligent,
and sometimes arrogant or aggressive, *unassurance*.

Let us examine, from this point of view, one of the
short poems from *Lustra*:

Like a skein of loose silk blown against a wall
    She walks by the railing of a path in
                            Kensington Gardens,
And she is dying piece-meal
                    of a sort of emotional anaemia.

And round about there is a rabble
Of the filthy, sturdy, unkillable infants
                                    of the very poor.
They shall inherit the earth.

In her is the end of breeding.
Her boredom is exquisite and excessive.
She would like some one to speak to her,
And is almost afraid that I
                        will commit that indiscretion.[10]

One can, again, see in that poem anticipations of the
early manner of Eliot. The "unromantic" simile, drawn
from the works of man not from the glories of nature,
"Like a skein of loose silk blown against a wall," seems to
anticipate Eliot's famous, more violent and surprising
simile (for sunset), at the beginning of "Prufrock," "Like
a patient etherised upon a table." This is not, though
many of the poems in *Lustra* are, a pure imagist poem; it
is impressionism, with satirical-sentimental comment.
And the diction is that of the highbrow, being deliberately
informal. In the phrase "of a sort of emotional anaemia,"
the words "sort of" are demotic, the words "emotional
anaemia" mandarin; but "emotional anaemia" is slightly
demotic also: the highbrow formula, the cultural slang,
of a period, used with a certain self-critical irony. Again,
notice the contrast of the very direct, very demotic line,
"She would like some one to speak to her," with the again
ironically self-critical use of mandarin speech in the
phrase, "will commit that indiscretion." A highly precarious and artificial language, in this little poem, reaches
a convincing temporary balance. And the feelings behind
the little poem are balanced also, of course, with the same
precarious elegance.

As impressionist, rather than imagist, this little poem
is not typical of *Lustra*. The more typical poems are of two
lines, four lines, six lines: developing separately, or some-

times fusing, what Pound had learned from the Japanese
tradition of imagism, from the *haiku*, and from the Greek
anthology but even more from the epigrams of Martial.
Pound shows hardly any sense of *wit* in his poems before
Lustra: at the best, instead of wit, he displays a schoolboy facetiousness or a boisterous jocularity. But the
poems in *Lustra* are full of wit. Here are some admirable
epigrams:

EPITAPH

Leucis, who intended a Grand Passion,
　　Ends with a willingness-to-oblige.[12]

Or a couple of lines from "Salvationists":

Come, my songs, let us speak of perfection—
We shall get ourselves rather disliked.[13]

Or "Phyllidula":

Phyllidula is scrawny but amorous,
Thus have the gods awarded her,
That in pleasure she receives more than she can give;
If she does not count this blessed
Let her change her religion.[11]

Or "The Patterns":

Erinna is a model parent,
Her children have never discovered her adulteries.
Lalage is also a model parent,
Her offspring are fat and happy.[14]

The technique there is reticence, implication. Occasion-
ally, however, in *Lustra*, Pound combines the bite of the
epigram in Martial's tradition with Japanese imagistic
techniques: as in "The Encounter":

D   E.P.

All the while they were talking the new morality
Her eyes explored me.
And when I arose to go
Her fingers were like the tissue
Of a Japanese paper napkin.[15]

I do not know whether any critic of Pound, other than myself, shares the pleasure which I have felt, over a period of about twenty years, in these tiny brilliant poems. William Empson once said to me that the poems in *Lustra* would be good little observations to put into a novel but were too slight to stand by themselves; I find one goes back to them, all the same.

The early examples of pure imagism, nearly pure *haiku* technique, are more important, as inventions, and for their influence. As I discovered when I was teaching English in Japan, the Japanese find much Western poetry prosaic; in the *haiku* there are no abstract statements, no direct expressions of personal emotion; everything is implied by images and the order of images:

The old pond, yes, and
A frog jumping into the
Water, and a splash!

That famous *haiku* of Basho's, like a pebble dropping into a pond, may spread around it ever widening rings; there is stillness, and then an event that breaks the stillness, and then more permanently the stillness again. But to make that kind of abstract reflexion *in* the poem (as Wordsworth, for instance, often makes such reflexions) would seem in the classical Japanese tradition heavy and vulgar. Pound's most famous short imagist poem was inspired by seeing the faces of two or three beautiful girls in a drab crowd in a Paris underground station. He wrote a poem about this experience in thirty lines or so, cut it down to ten lines, finally cut it down to two: one image superimposed on another: the little poem is called "In a Station of the Metro":

> The apparition of these faces in the crowd:
> Petals on a wet, black bough.[16]

The line "Petals on a wet, black bough" is not, in the traditional sense, a metaphor: it is rather that two images are juxtaposed, the beautiful faces in the dense, drab crowd, the blossoms on the black, wet branch, and suddenly a kind of electric current runs between them.

What would traditionally be called the metaphor or simile can come first in such a short poem: as in "Alba":

> As cool as the pale wet leaves
> of lily-of-the-valley
> She lay beside me in the dawn.[17]

Or the last line of a still short but more detailed impressionistic poem can carry this short of shock: as in "Liu Ch'e":

> The rustling of the silk is discontinued,
> Dust drifts over the court-yard,
> There is no sound of foot-fall, and the leaves
> Scurry into heaps and lie still,
> And she the rejoicer of the heart is beneath them:
> A wet leaf that clings to the threshold.[18]

Other slightly different techniques in *Lustra* look towards some of the techniques of the *Cantos*: for instance, a technique of intensification by repetition. In a little poem called "Ione, Dead the Long Year," no phrase is memorable in itself; the lingering of the voice in repetition, the sad slow dwelling on a dying cadence, makes all the memorableness:

> Empty are the ways,
> Empty are the ways of this land
> And the flowers
> Bend over with heavy heads.

Empty are the ways of this land
Where Ione
Walked once, and now does not walk
But seems like a person just gone.[19]

The technical inventions of *Lustra* are carried on later in *Cathay*: as in "Separation on the River Kiang":

Ko-jin goes west from Ko-kaku-ro.
The smoke-flowers are blurred over the river.
His lone sail blots the far sky.
And now I see only the river,
        The long Kiang, reaching heaven.[20]

Or one could quote "Taking Leave of a Friend," also from *Cathay*:

Blue mountains to the north of the walls,
White river winding about them;
Here we must make separation
And go out through a thousand miles of dead grass.

Mind like a floating wide cloud,
Sunset like the parting of old acquaintances
Who bow over their clasped hands at a distance.
Our horses neigh to each other
        as we are departing.[21]

What Pound learned from his imagist period (and what is perhaps permanently valuable in imagism) was a technique of cleanly isolating an impression or an emotion, cutting it free from comment, and a technique also of shaping verse cadences, and verse pauses, to the impression or emotion; instead of, as it were, feeding the impression of the emotion into a predetermined verse form.

I have described in the first chapter of this book the genesis of *Cathay*. When Pound wrote *Cathay* in 1915, and

when he worked up Fenollosa's notes on, and versions of,
Japanese Noh plays in 1916, he did not, in a sense that
any scholar would recognise, "know" either Chinese or
Japanese. Fenollosa, as I have said, was primarily a
scholar of Japanese art and literature, and the names of
poets and places in his notes were given in their Japanese
form. Thus Rihaku is the Japanese form of the Chinese
name Li-Po. Even a reader who has a mere smattering
of knowledge about Chinese and Japanese should recognise that the place-name in the beautiful line,

> Ko-Jin goes west from Ko-kaku-ro,

must be Japanese, because Chinese words are monosyllables or combinations of monosyllables, and because
there is no *r* in Chinese phonetics, just as there is no *l* in
Japanese phonetics.

It is almost incredible in these circumstances that the
versions in *Cathay* should not be wildly inaccurate, but
apparently they are not; *Cathay* has not been replaced as
a window for English-speaking readers into the classical
Chinese world even by the versions of Arthur Waley, who
is a true poet, and a very great scholar (as not the warmest admirer of Pound would ever claim that Pound is).
Perhaps Pound in his greatest translations, or rehandlings, is always *more* than a translator. He is at his best as a
translator when the theme of his original brings his own
deepest feelings into play: as in these lines from one of the
poems of exile in *Cathay*:

> What is the use of talking, and there is
> > no end of talking.
> There is no end of things in the heart.
> I call in the boy,
> Have him sit on his knees here
> > To seal this,
> And send it a thousand miles, thinking.[22]

In Pound's later work, the memory of the meeting and the parting of friends, the remembering of friends at a distance are also some of the most insistent themes, and the most movingly handled; one thinks, for instance, of the reminiscences of Yeats, of Hulme, and of humbler friends of the London days, now forgotten, in the *Pisan Cantos*. What a poet of Pound's power and originality perhaps ultimately does find in the poetry of other times and languages is his own preoccupations, his own vision, himself.

For instance, when we read these lines, with their breath-taking magnificence, from Pound's "Seafarer,"

> Days little durable,
> And all the arrogance of earthen riches,
> There come now no kings nor Caesars
> Nor gold-giving lords like those gone.
> Howe'er in mirth most magnified,
> Whoe'er lived in life most lordliest,
> Drear all this excellence, delights undurable!
> Waneth the watch, but the world holdeth.
> Tomb hideth trouble. The blade is layed low. . . .[23]

we feel that it would be merely pedantic if we pointed out that the true sense of the phrase Pound renders as "earthen riches" is "earthly kingdoms"; that it would be petty to suggest that if Pound wants us to pronounce "Caesars" as "Kaisers," as he obviously does, he ought not to rely on our having learned the modern pronunciation of Latin at school; and that it would be obtuse to object that the splendid line,

> Waneth the watch, but the world holdeth,

though it wonderfully represents the sound of the original, completely misrepresents the sense; which is "The weak live on"—the word which Pound mistranslates as "waneth" is the Old English ancestor of a verb used by Chaucer, "woneth," dwelleth—"and hold the earth."

What is important is that a version like Pound's "Seafarer" is a more actual influence on modern poetry than (unfortunately or otherwise) its original is ever likely to be. In his introduction to Pound's *Selected Poems*, Eliot, praising *Cathay*, pointed out that we today read the great Tudor translations, Florio's Montaigne or North's Plutarch, more as part of the English literature of their own age than as a guide to the books they translated. The seeming transparency of some great translations can never be more than a contemporary illusion; with every large change of idiom, the job has to be done over again. It is as a durable addition to, and influence upon, original poetry in the English language in this century—English including, of course, American-English and, because of Pound's great influence on the most important living Scottish poet, Hugh MacDiarmid, Scottish-English and Lowland Scots—that Pound's translations will be finally valued. They are poems in their own right, starting from something in a foreign language, and perhaps getting startlingly far away from it; they are not cribs.

The poems I have been dealing with so far have, apart from "The Seafarer" and from *Cathay*, considered as in a sense a single poem, an impression of classical China, been short, and often slight. I would now like to consider Pound's three most ambitious and important long poems before his major opus, the *Cantos*. These three poems are "Near Perigord," *Hugh Selwyn Mauberley*, and "Homage to Sextus Propertius." They are grouped in the English collected shorter poems as "Poems from Lustra (1915)" though later on in the contents list the third of them is given as "Homage to Sextus Propertius (1917)." (The *exact* dating of Pound's individual poems is a task for somebody with gifts for bibliographical scholarship which I do not possess. The Great War comes directly into *Hugh Selwyn Mauberley* and, in an indirect way, very

powerfully influences the anti-imperialist irony of
"Homage to Sextus Propertius." I would guess that
"Near Perigord," Pound's last important "Pre-Raphaelite" poem, may have been written before the outbreak of
the Great War.)

"Near Perigord," though I think it is a very good
poem indeed, has not, so far as I know, been criticised in
great detail. It is the successful culmination of Pound's
essays in a late Pre-Raphaelite vein, his translations from
Provençal and from Cavalcanti, his exercises, suggesting
William Morris or Rossetti or some aspects of Swinburne,
in medieval local colour. Behind it, however, more importantly, lies a non-Pre-Raphaelite poet, Robert
Browning. Pound was born in the Victorian age, his
early heroes were Victorian poets, and "Near Perigord"
uses Victorian technical inventions: dramatic mono-
logue; dramatisation within lyricism: the use of a narra-
tive-reflective framework, with lyrical interludes, to state
and to try to solve a moral problem. The major Victorian
poets, whom it is the fashion to dismiss as representing the
decadence of romanticism, ought to be recognised, as an
architect like Butterfield is now recognised, as very great
if very queer technical inventors: and "Near Perigord"
I would call a great late-Victorian poem.

It is about the troubadour Bertrans de Born, whose
lament for the young English King Pound had translated earlier. Bertrans de Born comes into Dante's Hell,
as a stirrer up of strife. He loved war; he egged the sons
of Henry II to fight against their father. He wrote a
famous and obscure love poem, celebrating all the aristo-
cratic married ladies in his neighbourhood and saying
that the lady, Maent, to whom the poem was addressed
combined all their various beauties (this one's com-
plexion, that one's hair, the other's nice manners).
Scholars have worried whether this was a sincere love
poem or part of a complicated piece of tactics, to win
friends and to divide enemies—to create good-will here,

jealousy there, among the ladies (and ultimately among the lords) of neighbouring castles. That is the problem which Pound in the first section of the poem tackles in a very Browningesque way? What can one really know about the past anyway:

> What is Sir Bertrans' singing?
> Maent, Maent, and yet again Maent,
> Or war and broken heaumes and politics?[24]

The second section of the poem begins with the words, "End fact. Try fiction." It gives a series of glimpses of Bertrans or his friends or enemies and the manner now suggests less Browning than, say, William Morris: Pre-Raphaelite word-painting:

> The tents tight drawn, horses at tether
> Farther and out of reach, the purple night,
> The crackling of small fires, the bannerets.
> The lazy leopards on the largest banner,
> Stray gleams on hanging mail, an armourer's torch-flare
> Melting on steel. . . .[25]

The glimpses, however, leave the moral problem unsolved. Bertrans is dead, and Richard Coeur de Lion and the troubadour Arnaut Daniel discuss him:

> 'Do we know our friends?'
> 'Say that he saw the castles, say that he loved Maent!'
> 'Say that he loved her, does it solve the riddle?'[26]

Richard is shot, Arnaut dies, we are left with no evidence except Dante's great lines, magnificently rendered:

> Surely I saw, and still before my eyes
> Goes on that headless trunk, that bears for light
> Its own head swinging, gripped by the dead hair,
> And like a swinging lamp that says, 'Ah me!
> I severed men, my head and heart
> Ye see here severed, my life's counterpart.'[27]

But the poem, wonderfully impressive so far as a revival of Victorian modes, reaches its greatness in the third section. Speculation and historical reconstruction have left Pound baffled. In the last section, he solves his problem by letting Bertrans himself speak; letting him explain the nature and the tragedy of his love for Maent. One of Pound's finest sustained pieces of verse, carrying in a single movement lyrical impetus, the thrust and colour of narrative, the shock of deep perception, the third section of "Near Perigord" deserves quoting in full:

Bewildering spring, and by the Auvezere
Poppies and day's eyes in the green émail
Rose over us; and we knew all that stream,
And our two horses had traced out the valleys;
Knew the low flooded lands squared out with poplars,
In the young days when the deep sky befriended.
    And great wings beat above us in the twilight,
And the great wheels in heaven
Bore us together . . . surging . . . and apart . . .
Believing we could meet with lips and hands,

    High, high, and sure . . . and then the counter-thrust:
'Why do you love me? Will you always love me?
But I am like the grass, I can not love you!'
Or, 'Love, and I love and love you,
And hate your mind, not *you*, your soul, your hands.'

      So to this last estrangement, Tairiran!

      There shut up in his castle, Tairiran's,
She who had nor ears nor tongue save in her hands,
Gone—ah, gone—untouched, unreachable!
She who could never live save through one person,
She who could never speak save to one person,
And all the rest of her a shifting change,
A broken bundle of mirrors. . . . ![28]

The setting of this very fine poem is medieval, but what should be noticed is how the psychology is basically romantic-Victorian—one thinks of Browning's "Last Ride Together," even of the love situations in some of Tennyson's "Idylls of the King"—and in the special kind of selfconsciousness depicted in the passage just quoted most unmedieval; but in spite of the Victorian feel of the thing as a whole the last brilliant image of "a shifting change, A broken bundle of mirrors . . ." takes us forward to the modern age, Pound's own age, in which total images are analysed, fragmented, put together to look different—the age of Cubism and Vorticism, the age of Eliot's exploration of "the limits of coherency" (the phrase of an early reviewer in *The Times Literary Supplement*) in *The Waste Land*. "Historical" poetry, like the "historical" novel, ultimately throws much more light on the age in which it is written than on the age which it is written about. The moral question about Bertrans in this poem is, of course, the moral question about Pound. Should he, too, be condemned as a stirrer up of strife? Is it the Muse he has loved, or opinion and self-will?—

> What is Sir Bertrans' singing?
> Maent, Maent, and yet again Maent,
> Or war and broken heaumes and politics?[29]

One should notice also that the kind of relationship between a man and a woman which Pound sketches in the passage quoted is that often dealt with, not so romantically, or not with this kind of "literary" romanticism, by D. H. Lawrence: body-soul affinity, mental antagonism. Lawrence would have appreciated the theme of a woman's need for dependence (her sense of not being a self or a being outside the male orbit) tensed against repulsion, the need for being oneself. Another theme of Lawrence's is also implicit, the danger of excessive "spirituality" or "spiritual consciousness" in a love relationship. But Pound, though he praised the handling of

dialect in some of Lawrence's early poems, praised their
Hardyesque aspect, with his conscious mind violently
rejected Lawrence's attitude to life. What is Lawrentian
in this poem is something absorbed unconsciously, something in the air of the 1910's.

If "Near Perigord" is the crown of the Victorian aspect
of Pound's talent, *Hugh Selwyn Mauberley* is Pound's first
completely "modern" poem: Dr Leavis, for instance,
thinks the earlier poems mainly important in so far as
they lead up to *Mauberley*, and Eliot in his introduction to
the *Selected Poems* sees, also, the concentration and the
freedom of the handling of verse in *Mauberley* as the re-
ward of years of patient craftsmanship, of apprenticeship
to strict techniques. *Mauberley* in Pound's general opus
has the same place as *The Waste Land* in Eliot's; it is, so to
say, his diploma piece. It is, in a way, the same sort of
poem: a commentary on, a vision of, the fragmentation
of contemporary civilisation. I used to think a large part
of its importance lay in the fact that, essentially, it made
The Waste Land possible; Eliot's dedication of that poem
to Pound as *il miglior fabbro* I interpreted in my own mind
as being to the better craftsman, rather than to the better
artist. I now think *Mauberley* a better poem than *The
Waste Land*. I feel that one could say about *The Waste
Land* more or less what Eliot says, himself, about *Hamlet*:
that it is extraordinarily and permanently "interesting"
rather than being a really satisfying art-work; that there
is a submerged powerful set of feelings behind it which
do not find an "objective correlative." It is not really
a poem about the crack-up of a culture or the decay of
faith. The more one re-reads it, and like *Hamlet* it bears
continual re-reading, the more it seems to be centrally
and even obsessively a poem about sexual failure. The
typist, the rich young couple, the woman who has had an
abortion and her horrid friend, the girls seduced by the
loitering heirs of city directors, the girls seduced in punts
or canoes, they are all doing it, or have done it, and not

one of the poor things seems to get the least bit of a kick
out of it. And were poor old Elizabeth and Leicester in
much better case? I think the basic emotion behind *The
Waste Land* is the horror of a child or a young adolescent,
before our own era, when we are more sensible about
these things, on discovering "the facts of life": my father
does that to my mother, no, it cannot be. This is probably
wildly unjust. But I would be willing to argue at more
length that *The Waste Land* is not really a poem about the
general culture, and its state: *Mauberley* is, and a very
fine poem, indeed.

Hugh Selwyn Mauberley can be seen, broadly, as Pound's
farewell, at once wistful and ironic, to a purely "aesthetic"
attitude to poetry. His farewell is to the idea that one can
make a cult of "beauty," and in a minor degree of "love"
and of "pleasure," in indifference to, or in quiet defiance
of, a greedily competitive and in the end violently self-
destructive society. (The Great War is a central datum
of the poem.) Mauberley, the "hero" of the poem, is not
wholly Pound; but he is a real aspect of Pound. The note
is set in the opening poem of *Mauberley*, "E.P. Ode Pour
L'Election de son Sepulchre":

> His true Penelope was Flaubert,
> He fished by obstinate isles;
> Observed the elegance of Circe's hair
> Rather than the mottoes on sun-dials.[30]

Flaubert is the type of the saint and martyr of literature,
the man who has not a life of his own apart from his work
but squeezes his life drop by drop into it; who gives to
literature a devotion and concentration, Mauriac has
suggested, that are excessive for that object, that ought to
belong to God. He is the patron saint of aestheticism, and
Pound ought to have rejoined him in Ithaca, but he has
instead spent his time fishing by the islands of pleasure,
like that of Circe in the Odyssey, which prevent him
from reaching his Ithaca. (They are obstinate, I think,

because in one's youth they will not allow one to pass them by.) A hedonistic-aesthetic attitude to female beauty ("observed the elegance of Circe's hair") has absorbed Pound so much that he has not noticed the mottoes on sundials: such mottoes, for instance, as "It is later than you think."

Mauberley, rather exceptionally among Pound's poems, is a poem full of adult self-criticism. He recognises that he has lacked sufficient artistic concentration because he has not, so far, been sufficiently aware of the strength and pervasiveness of the "shoddy cheapness" in his age, a cheapness armed against him:

> The age demanded an image
> Of its accelerated grimace. . . .
> The "age demanded" chiefly a mould in plaster
>
> Made with no loss of time,
> A prose kinema, not, not assuredly, alabaster
> Or the "sculpture" of rhyme.[31]

We can apply that, with terrible precision, to what contemporaries of Pound were reading or writing: the non-art, "social" or "documentary" novels of Wells, Galsworthy, Bennett; the long verse narratives of John Masefield; the loose writing in prose and verse of Chesterton; the prefaces of Shaw; some of the prose, at least, of Belloc; some of the verse, at least, of Kipling. These were all decent men, sincerely devoted to what they sincerely believed to be the best causes; but the ear of the public preoccupied them more than thoughts of the high, stern, difficult integrity of art. Indeed, art, since the 1890's, since the Oscar Wilde scandal, had become rather a dirty word; it still is, on the whole, in English universities, where it is becoming a kind of unspoken imperative that one must always discuss literature primarily in terms of "moral values."

Pound wrote *Mauberley* at the beginning, over the first two years, of the Great War. His reflexions on the standards of contemporary civilisation lead him to ask what exactly it is that "a myriad,/And of the best, among them," are dying for:

> Charm, smiling at the good mouth,
> Quick eyes gone under earth's lid
>
> For two gross of broken statues,
> For a few thousand battered books.[39]

The "statues" and "books" are, of course, or represent, what Pound himself has so far mainly cared for: the literary and artistic culture handed down from the past, kept in being by the integrity of scholars and the enthusiasm of amateurs, kept in being by a minority. He notices now that the "statues" and the "books" are not notably transforming the general quality of lived life. They are not a dominant impulse; they are something for museums.

Pound therefore feels (the war is not the subject of his poem, but brought in as a kind of touchstone, to raise the question what is worth dying for) that he is living in a killingly philistine age. But to "distance" his treatment of this age, to make it objective, he makes the hero of his poem, not himself, but somebody rather like himself, but weaker, an essentially minor artist and a necessarily defeated man, as Pound is not. Hugh Selwyn Mauberley, as a person, is the pure aesthete, looking back on the prolonged defeat of the aesthetic movement in England, of Rossetti and the Pre-Raphaelites, of the poets, later, of the Rhymers' Club. The poem "Yeux Glauques," for instance, is about the Pre-Raphaelites.

It uses, as Pound is also to use in the *Cantos*, historical personages as emblems of, personifications of, something much wider than themselves. There is no name (though

it is covered by some of the meanings of the word "allusion") for this device, which is one of Pound's main
innovating devices. It is not symbolism; it is not imagism.
It is the use of an historical proper name, or more rarely
one out of myth or legend, to stand not for one abstract
idea but for a cluster of attitudes. It depends very much,
of course, on the reader sharing Pound's historical knowledge and either intuitively sympathising with, or guessing
and adjusting himself to, Pound's attitudes.

Here is an example from "Yeux Glauques": I will call
the device cluster-evocation:

> Gladstone was still respected
> When John Ruskin produced
> "King's Treasuries"; Swinburne
> And Rossetti still abused.
>
> Foetid Buchanan lifted up his voice
> When that faun's head of hers
> Became a pastime for
> Painters and adulterers. . . .[33]

What are the clusters there? Gladstone probably stands
for Pound not, as for many of us, for the high and serious
morality of Victorian politics at their best, but for pom-
pousness and humbug; and yet the view of Gladstone
taken here will certainly not be identical with the view
taken, say, by Lytton Strachey in *Eminent Victorians*.
Pound was writing at a time when Asquith, the last
Gladstonian in British politics, was being edged out of
power, and when Lloyd George, whom Pound detested,
was edging into power. Gladstone was at least a classical
scholar, he translated Homer. The age that respected
him, though it was perhaps wrong not to see through an
element of sheer cloudiness in the G.O.M., would be
better for Pound than the age that respected Lloyd
George; it had at least a certain care for outward de-
corum.

Ruskin similarly stands for a noble and pathetic, because failed, attempt to link the values of art to the values of society. Like Gladstone, he was a stern Victorian moralist; but, unlike Gladstone, he understood what Swinburne and Rossetti were up to. "Foetid Buchanan" is the Scottish journalist and embittered failed poet, who had tried to launch David Gray on London as a Scottish Keats. Out of spite and jealousy, he wrote a famous pamphlet, *The Fleshly School of Poetry*, accusing the Pre-Raphaelites generally, and Rossetti particularly, of disguising mere sensuality as spirituality. He stands for Victorian philistinism, but without Gladstone's personal nobility, Victorian strait-lacedness, but without Ruskin's homage to art. What he had in his case is admitted in

> When that faun's head of hers
> Became a pastime for
> Painters and adulterers. . . .[34]

The faun's head is, say, Elizabeth Siddal's, the typical pale swooning Pre-Raphaelite beauty, but also the Muse's, the White Goddess's; her votaries are adulterers both in that, from Buchanan's point of view, they lead immoral lives, and from her own that their devotion to her is betrayed by self-destructive weakness. The Pre-Raphaelites and still more the Decadents lack Ruskin's sense that order in art must spring from moral order, from order in social life. So they destroy themselves:

> Dowson found harlots cheaper than hotels . . .

And for the typical philistine-artist of the Edwardian age, for Mr Nixon, who is Arnold Bennett, they are merely awful warnings: he warns Pound or Mauberley,

> "And no one knows, at sight, a masterpiece.
> And give up verse, my boy,
> There's nothing in it."[35]

He advises him also:

> "Butter reviewers. From fifty to three hundred
> I rose in eighteen months;
> The hardest nut I had to crack
> Was Dr Dundas."[36]

"Dr Dundas" was very probably the Scottish editor of
The British Weekly, the leading Nonconformist journal of
the Edwardian age; a son of an Aberdeenshire manse,
Robertson Nicoll, who wrote readable little essays under
the name "Claudius Clear." He reviewed the same book,
habitually, so often in different places that Conan Doyle
once accused him of being a conspiracy; he replied that
he wrote to make money, and wished he could make as
much as Conan Doyle. He was not a contemptible man:
he was a fine scholar, a writer of clear plain prose,
genuinely religious in his way (though, as a Scottish
Presbyterian, he intellectually despised the English
Nonconformists whom he wrote for), a man whose shrewd
and disinterested advice was sought by leading states-
men; similarly Bennett, or Mr Nixon, was at his best an
artist, and a fine one.

Pound's point, in all this potted and allusive cultural
history in *Mauberley*, is a double one: in an age dominated
by the quest for wealth and power, even people with the
capacity for art and thought betray the best that is in
them; and the artist who merely turns away in disgust
from that quest, from society's general pattern, destroys
himself, and feeds himself during the process of self-
destruction on fantasy:

> Told me how Johnson (Lionel) died
> By falling from a high stool in a pub. . . .
>
> But showed no trace of alcohol
> At the autopsy, privately performed—
> Tissue preserved—the pure mind
> Arose toward Newman as the whisky warmed.[37]

The extraordinary just balance of *Mauberley* is one of the things that makes it a great poem. Apart from sheer brutal philistinism, an Edwardian aesthete like Mauberley has to contend with the kind of fashionable, patronising interest in literature of the English aristocracy, which is partly a kind of "slumming," partly a way of making oneself interesting: as in Pound's passage on the Lady Valentine (Ottoline Morell?):

> Poetry, her border of ideas,
> The edge, uncertain, but a means of blending
> With other strata
> Where the lower and higher have ending;
>
> A hook to catch the Lady Jane's attention,
> A modulation toward the theatre,
> Also, in the case of revolution,
> A possible friend and comforter.[38]

Notice that the social satire here is entirely valid and probably perennially contemporary; I have met Mr Nixon, or his modern versions; and the Lady Valentine.

Mauberley's weakness, what Pound is centrally probing for, is that he is a *minor* artist, narrow in his scope, lacking the kind of energy of the great creative Renaissance artists, the energy that would have enabled him to transform his age:

> Firmness,
> Not the full smile,
> His art, but an art
> In profile;
>
> Colourless
> Pier Francesca,
> Pisanello lacking the skill
> To forge Achaia.[39]

One of the most learned of contemporary English poets, Constantine Trypanis, Professor of Byzantine and Modern Greek studies at Oxford, once, in a lecture of his which I attended, quoted these lines as an example of beautifully modulated verse containing no clear sense or drift. But using my tool of cluster-evocation, and reading the lines in their total context, sense and drift, of course, are perfectly clear. If Mauberley *had been* Pisanello, his art would have had colour—body, fullness, impact—as well as clarity of line; he *would have had* the skill to "forge Achaia," to make the classical world come alive again in bronze or marble, the skill which the men of the Renaissance had. But his gifts are narrower, his "tool The engraver's" (line, black and white, the burin biting the steel plate, the possibility of style, but a style implying stiffness and narrowness; no colour, no free calligraphy).

And the concentration needed for even such a narrow and minor art (the engraver's, not even the etcher's, which allows a scribbly line) Mauberley loses by entangling himself in a love affair and drifting through life in a state of mainly passive, though up to a point discriminatingly passive, hedonism. Deserted by his mistress,

> Unable in the supervening blankness
> To sift TO AGATHON from the chaff
> Until he found his sieve . . .
> Ultimately his seismograph:[40]

Tὸ ἀγαθόν, the good, the noble, the beautiful, some kind of ultimate value or beauty: and the very passivity of Mauberley to experience (Wordsworth's "wise passiveness," Keats's "negative capability") ultimately becomes his seismograph—an instrument for recording deep or distant earth tremors on rolls of moving paper with a sensitive moving needle; it becomes his method of making an exact record of social and aesthetic, and most profoundly perhaps of his own inner emotional, change. But Mauberley, wounded by love, is in a kind of daze. He had

aimed at the art of engravings or medallions, at transforming "the relation/Of eye-lid and cheek-bone/By
verbal manifestations," but

> He had passed, inconscient, full gaze,
> The wide-banded irides
> And botticellian sprays implied
> In their diastasis.[41]

In such a stanza, though hardly ever earlier, and not often
later, Pound is difficult in precisely the manner of William
Empson (or of some of Ronald Bottrall's early poems,
though these, unlike Empson's, often come directly out of
a Poundian influence). I looked up the French equivalent
for diastasis in Littré, and found this which, I hope
accurately, I translate:

Accidental separation of two articulated bones:
chemical meaning, a soluble fermenting agent that
transforms various substances: ptyalin in the salivary
glands is diastatic.

Mauberley needed for his "verbal manifestations" the
wide-banded (large) irises of women's eyes (but one
should not ignore Iris the rainbow-goddess, or iris the
flower). Dazed by lost love, he had passed these irises by.
Diastasis therefore could be a very learned way of refer-
ring to the apparition of two irises on either side of the
nose (the nose would be the stalk of the "botticellian
sprays"!); or, in the other sense, not that of "separation
of two articulated bones," diastasis could be the transforming, magical effect of the gaze of a beautiful woman,
working a chemical change on the emotions, as the saliva
works such a change on food.

The iris (eye)—iris (flower) pun, here, helps to prop
the comparison of Mauberley to a botanist who has
somehow failed to pick out his prize specimen. Mauberley
is thought of at this stage in the poem as the man who has
given up the struggle to *create* art, who has surrendered

himself to a life of sensation. Passive sensation itself
almost automatically discriminates: but Mauberley dis-
covers that he has found his great prize orchid—the true
emotion, the aesthetic correspondence of feeling and
object, Eliot's "objective correlative," the shopgirl's "Mr
Right"—too late. In a state of dazedness ("anaesthesis")
he has by-passed the possible grand emotion ("affect"):

> Which anaesthesis, noted a year late,
> And weighed, revealed his great affect,
> (Orchid), mandate
> Of Eros, a retrospect. . . .[42]

Mauberley is left with "mouths biting empty air," sym-
bols of catatonic paranoia, almost, of frustrated desire
frozen into grotesque images of paralysed rage and terror.

Mauberley's tragedy is (to refine a little on a point
which Dr F. R. Leavis was the first to make) the tragedy,
or tragi-comedy, of the *pure* aesthete, for whom even the
effort to *make*, let alone the effort to *act* (the reader will
remember Miss Arendt's distinctions between contemplation, action, making, and labour) in the end seems a
brutal and unnecessary disturbance of the delights of
pure, passive contemplation. And this passivity, which is
his purity, his fine discriminating instrument, is also his
helplessness and his defencelessness. He is seen, meta-
phorically, it is not part of his "story," as a castaway on a
raft in the South Seas, too much delighted with what he pas-
sively perceives to wish to record it, to wish even to make
for land and save his life. He has reached an earthly paradise, of sorts, and perhaps all earthly paradises are lethal:

> A pale gold, in the aforesaid pattern,
> The unexpected palms
> Destroying, certainly, the artist's urge,
> Left him delighted with the imaginary
> Audition of the phantasmal sea-surge . . .[43]

But there are things to admire in him. He did in the end

write one brilliantly hard, artificial little Gautierian poem, which Pound gives us at the end of *Mauberley*; he did attain an almost Buddhistic inner placidity; defeated, always, through an undefended fineness, he was never vulgar, never malicious, never corrupt. "Mildness amid the neo-Nietzschean clatter": that is Mauberley's moral note, queerly different in some ways, from the later moral note of Pound himself.

Mauberley has a very central place in Pound's work. It has been much praised. The last long poem before the *Cantos*, "Homage to Sextus Propertius," has had a much more chequered critical history. T. S. Eliot decided not to include it in the *Selected Poems*. Latin scholars have pointed out with glee various startling howlers in this poem, if it is to be considered as a straight version of poems by, and passages from, Propertius. Robert Graves has made brilliant fun of a defence of the poem which I published, some years ago, in an anonymous review of the English edition of Pound's collected verse translations. I had better say that I am not a very good linguist. I have no Greek. My Latin is up to Scottish first year university standard, and though I have done versions of poems by Catullus, Horace, and Ovid that have pleased good scholars, I have done them always with the aid of a crib. I can read and have translated from French, Spanish, and Italian, but speak all these languages very incorrectly, only partly follow conversations in them, and could not write in them. I know a great deal about the structure of the Japanese and Chinese languages, but cannot read more than a few of the Chinese characters in which both are written. Yet I feel it is not impossible, even with this smattering, amateur equipment to get at something, cadence, rhythm, general structure, images, in poems in languages one only imperfectly understands; thus I have a sympathy with Pound's exercises in translation, which is not all shared, for instance, by a severe and exact scholar like Robert Graves.

Let me repeat here some of the remarks of which
Graves made such excellent fun. The case of the scholars
against Pound as a translator is that he perpetually shows
signs of not knowing properly the languages he is translating from. Even where he must be presumed to know
the sense of his originals, such critics declare, Pound often,
for his own rhetorical purposes in English, distorts this
sense in a wilful and unnecessary way. Pound did not, in
fact, include "Homage to Sextus Propertius" in the
English volume of his collected translations. It is not
strictly a translation, but rather what a Restoration poet
would have called an "Allusion to Propertius" or "Imitation of Propertius"; what Pound himself would call a
persona. Scholars, nevertheless, are right in finding howlers
in the poem. They could discover howlers also, for instance, in Marlowe's very beautiful versions of Ovid's
Amores. And it must be admitted that Pound's knowledge
of Latin, perhaps of most languages other than English,
is nearer to that of an eager undergraduate (an undergraduate impatient with grammar and in love with the
idea of poetry) than to that of a university lecturer. Yet
the scholars have largely missed Pound's point.

We can see what Pound is doing in this poem most
clearly if we look at passages where there are no howlers,
but where, for the sake of bringing out a latent irony,
Pound deliberately distorts or caricatures the strict sense.
Thus the elegiac couplet,

> a valeat, Phoebum quicumque moratur in armis!
>   exactus tenui pumice versus eat,

which is literally, in Butler's version, "Away with the
man who keeps Phoebus tarrying among the weapons of
war! Let verse run smoothly, polished with fine pumice,"
becomes in Pound's variation,

> Out-weariers of Apollo will, as we know, continue their
>   Martian generalities,
>   We have kept our erasers in order.[44]

Pound obviously here *does* understand the literal sense of the Latin. But, for his own purposes, he is "pointing up" that sense. But he is not using Propertius as a *mere* stalking-horse. He is, in the lines just quoted, striving by a slight distortion of the literal sense of his original to bring over more fully than Butler what he guesses to be its tone and feeling. He brings in "Martian" to remind us that it is a Latin poet he is starting from; the word "generalities," which has no equivalent in his original, is to reflect his own sense (which he imagines Propertius as sharing) that patriotic war poetry tends to be rhetorical in a bad sense, sonorously empty. On the other hand the word "erasers" (which suggests typewriter erasers to us much more immediately than it suggests fine pumice) reminds us that what Propertius is saying has for Pound himself a sharp contemporary relevance. The "out-weariers of Apollo" whom Pound is thinking of might include, say, Newbolt and Kipling.

This kind of distortion for contemporary relevance becomes much more marked in Pound's rendering of the lines,

> multi, Roma, tuas laudes annalibus addent,
> qui finem imperii Bactra futura canent;
> sed, quod pace legas, opus hoc de monte Sororum
> detulit intacta pagina nostra via.

Literally again, in Butler's version, these lines mean: "Many, O Rome, shall add fresh glories to thine annals, singing that Bactra shall be thine Empire's bound; but this work of mine my pages have brought down from the Muses' mount by an untrodden way, that thou mayest read it in the midst of peace." In "Homage to Sextus Propertius" this becomes, effectively, but certainly very surprisingly:

> Annalists will continue to record Roman reputations,
> Celebrities from the Trans-Caucasus will belaud
>   Roman celebrities

And expound the distentions of Empire,
But for something to read in normal circumstances?
For a few pages brought down from the forked hill
                                            unsullied?[45]

It does look here, at the first blush, as if Pound thought
that "annalibus" meant "by annalists" and even as if he
thought that "imperii Bactra" meant something like
legates or notabilities from Bactra, and was taking
"imperii" as a nominative plural noun, the subject of
"canent." On the other hand, the next line in his version,
"And expound the distentions of Empire" is obviously
based on a correct understanding of "qui finem imperii
. . . . canent." So it is best to assume that he is not blun-
dering, but deliberately emphasising the very faint note
of mockery of the official, patriotic Muse present in the
original. Just in the same way, the phrase, "But for
something to read in normal circumstances?" is an ex-
pansion, a heightening, of the discreet irony present in
the three words, "quod pace legas." In fact, for a very
discreet irony in the original, Pound substitutes a violent
satirical contempt. British Imperialism is probably far
more vividly in his mind than Roman Imperialism. The
"celebrities from the Trans-Caucasus" might be, for
instance, terribly old-hat patriotic poets from Canada or
Australia or New Zealand. "Homage to Sextus Propertius" works out, in fact, as a more "distanced" version of
Mauberley.

The hero is still the lyric poet, the pure artist, the lover,
disgusted by the violence and brassiness of Imperial
politics, slightly contemptuous of the fashionable and
immoral society women (Roman equivalents of the Lady
Valentine) who will, however, be a very important part
of his audience; aware, like Mauberley, of love largely in
terms of pain and loss; and, like Mauberley, or like
Pound, very much preoccupied with the thought of death,
and posthumous fame. The poem, as Eliot has pointed

out, is a wonderful exercise in various uses of rhythm; and the *persona* of Propertius allows Pound to experiment with longer, more sweeping lines than in *Mauberley* and with more fierce and direct expressions of feeling, of scorn, grief, tenderness, rage. As a poem fundamentally, like *Mauberley*, about Pound, Pound's world, "Homage to Sextus Propertius" seems to me a major achievement.

I now come to Ezra Pound's longest and most ambitious and still continuing work, the *Cantos*. The *Cantos* are a kind of epic, an attempt to revive the tradition of heroic narrative verse that will at once tell the "tale of the tribe" and keep the pride and courage of the tribe alive. But Pound's epic hero is not one particular man, like Odysseus, in quest of one particular place, Ithaca. It is man as such, or multifarious examples of him, in search of civilisation. This quest Pound sees as something like Odysseus's; Odysseus took ten years to get back to Ithaca, but Ithaca was where he had started from. And man's search for civilisation is, for Pound, a perpetual attempt to return to the first springs of skill or of delight. He celebrates, particularly, founders; the Provençal and early Italian poets, who created the tradition of European lyric poetry; the founders of modes of government or codes of behaviour, like Jefferson or Confucius; the kind of natural or primitive religious awe that is expressed, say, in Ovid's *Metamorphoses*, rather than the subtleties of Christian theology; the pioneering and reforming spirit, the spirit of individual adventure, rather than the sedateness of a mature society; the sages who tell anecdotes or utter precepts, like Confucious, rather than the sages, like Socrates, who engage in dialectic.

The *Cantos* are thus a highly selective view of history. Though he is celebrating civilisation, and high achievements in the arts and in other human skills as a mark of civilisation, Pound does not like, for instance, Elizabethan England (except for the song-writers), the age of Louis XIV, England or (except for Voltaire) France in the eighteenth century, or the nineteenth century much. The processes which have made civilisation growingly complicated, abstract thought, for instance, specialisations of various sorts, strike him as on the whole corrupting; he feels this specially, of course, about the power of finance, the international arms traffic, usury. A true civilisation, for Pound, respects the traditional rites and gods; sticks by sound laws and customs; its manners are marked by simplicity and directness, by naturalness, rather than pomp or artifice; it produces men with natural passions of which they are not ashamed, but also with public spirit, open minds, an alert curiosity. It creates stories and it creates, and fosters, art: it makes for a kind of abundance of life, and for the sense of natural magic. Odysseus, in his quest for this Ithaca, will confront many enemies, and many temptations; but some temptations, those which Pound typifies by Circe, are also rewards, and a kind of education. Ideally, the hero triumphs over difficulties, settles down to rule Ithaca justly, becomes a kind of cult hero for his tribe. But the tribe can never afford to stagnate. Man's task, as tribal hero, is one of perpetual renewal; and Pound, for instance, has no respect at all for an Austrian, a Metternichian kind of Conservatism. His heroes are renewers.

But the *Cantos* are not merely an attempt to create, say, the equivalent of Arnold Toynbee's *A Study of History* in verse. Pound's deepest mood is, I think, that of the Jeffersonian American radical; and in the *Cantos* that mood, with its simplicity and hopefulness, is confronted with the splendour, yes, but also with the violence, wastefulness, and destructiveness of European history. It is confronted, in some of the earlier cantos, especially with the impact of the Great War. Pound, it should be noticed, repeatedly uses the Odyssey in the *Cantos*, a tale of individual courage and resourcefulness; he makes no use at all of the Iliad, which Simone Weil calls "the poem of force." The Iliad suggests a tragic view; Pound has translated a play by Sophocles, but he does not like either Shakespeare or Racine, and the most centrally American thing about him is that the tragic view of life is alien to him. Tragedy was also an alien concept to the Middle Ages, except in so far as a "tragic" story illustrated falls from great estate, the turns of fortune's wheel. And Pound, using *The Divine Comedy* as he uses the Odyssey, can present with great honesty and huge impact an image of the violence, evil, decay in the world and yet move on to hope. In the earliest batch of *Cantos* there is a filthy hell of profiteers in which Pound seems personally trapped; but with the help of Blake, who acts suddenly as a kind of Virgil, he escapes; and the cantos immediately after the hell cantos, with their reminiscences of the Great War, and friends killed then, and their anecdotes about the arms traffic, represent the personal pressures behind the vivid horror of these cantos.

The first thirty cantos are the portion of the poem most likely to captivate a reader utterly indifferent to Pound's ideas. They contain some of Pound's most splendid translation or adaptation, from the Odyssey and from Ovid, and a beautifully vivid response both to the Mediterranean scene, effects of light and colour particularly, and to early Renaissance history, and Renaissance art. But the "matter of Europe" which they are mainly concerned with does end in the crack-up of the Great War; and in the subsequent cantos, up to *The Pisan Cantos* of 1948, Pound is increasingly didactic in his manner of procedure. He gives us cantos full of scraps of letters and official documents, lots of details about the Monte de Pietà in Siena or the fiscal reforms of the Grand Dukes of Tuscany, the Habsburg-Lorraine successors of the Medici, in the later eighteenth century. He devotes a whole set of cantos to the annals of China, as a country which has remained civilised for a very long time, because taxation has not been excessive, usury has not flourished, men have respected the Confucian code; and he devotes a similar long section to John Adams, the second President of the United States, and in a sense almost the father of a dynasty, as an example of what the good ruler, seeking to lay the foundations of a stable community, should be. These Adams cantos, which came out in 1940, are a great expression of American patriotism; it is tragic to think that their author, five years later, was nearly put on trial for his life for high treason.

The Pisan Cantos had been roughly drafted during Pound's imprisonment at Pisa, and were published, when he was an inmate of St Elizabeth's Hospital in Washington, in 1948. They did much to regain for Pound a general sympathy and interest which his political record had lost him. If one thinks of the pattern of *The Divine Comedy*, they are a kind of Purgatorio. Pound does not renounce any of his political ideas but his sufferings, and the collapse of all his hopes and fantasies, together bring out a human and personal note that is new. Pound's *personal* situation now is heroic, he is Odysseus; neither in Circe's island nor back in Ithaca nor making pleasant conversation with Nausicaa and her father; but, let us say, in Polyphemus' cave. He endures suffering and isolation not only bravely, but cheerfully, and gracefully; and in his isolation his mind goes back tenderly to old friends, Yeats, Elkin Mathews, Maurice Hewlett. He notices the birds—a great passage—perched on telephone wires like notes on a stave. He is grateful to the negro soldiers who give him a table and writing materials. There are passages of sustained and concentrated power (the elegy, in the metre of the Rubaiyat, for medieval and Tudor England, the portrait of Yeats, the great homily, "Cast down thy vanity") unmatched since the first thirty cantos; and there is a new humility, a touching realisation on Pound's part that he has not had enough pity for other people. There are the same old stubborn politics, but, however much one hates these, one almost admires Pound for not reneguing, *then*.

Purgatorio should be followed by a Paradiso, and many admirers of Pound see the subsequent two volumes of cantos, *Rock-Drill* and *Thrones*, as just that. I have not read *Thrones*, which is just out as I write; compared to *The Pisan Cantos*, *Rock-Drill* seems to me the writing of an old man, with a very full mind, but a mind that is perpetually betrayed into digression, and digression within digression; a single subject is rarely kept up for more than three or four lines at a time; and Pound is relying now much less on vivid evocation of scene and incident than on our remembering such evocations earlier in the *Cantos*.

In one of his interviews with D. G. Bridson Pound did, in fact, admit that *Rock-Drill* and *Thrones* would not make much sense to a reader who had not gone on the train earlier. Pound's voice is a wonderful voice to listen to even when it seems to be rambling on, without much direction, about anything that comes into Pound's head; but it does not now, to me at least, look as if the cantos still to come will do much to alter our general appreciation of the *Cantos*, or our judgment about their success as a total form. It *looks*, at least, as if Pound will go on writing cantos till he dies and that the paradisal element in them will be mainly the placidity, the easiness of voice and tone, which the old man has found after having undergone so much: though that of course is not, either morally or formally, nothing.

Any first reading of the *Cantos* is likely, even for many reasonably well-educated readers, to issue in bewilderment. The bewilderment (apart from one's ignorance of foreign languages) is often concerned more with what Pound is talking about than what he is saying. Let me mention a number of books or topics which I have myself found useful in tracking a way through the labyrinth. It is useful to have read something about Thomas Jefferson and Alexander Hamilton, and about the conflict between an ideal of agrarian democracy and a financial oligarchy centred in the cities which rises even at the beginnings of American history; one should know also about Andrew Jackson and Martin van Buren and their fight with the bank. It is important to realise that arguments about economics, about dear money and cheap money, have played a very important part in American history, and that in his absorption with economic problems Pound is not really, to a well-read American reader, eccentric; many of Pound's ideas about history and economics can be found, for instance, expressed in a simple and elegant prose very unlike Pound's in Brooks Adams's *The Law of Civilization and Decay*, published as long ago as 1896; and a modern English classic like R. H. Tawney's *Religion and the Rise of Capitalism* has its relevance to Pound's views on usury. Many of his general ideas on the proper relation of society and art are, like his admiration for Gothic and his dislike of Baroque, very reminiscent of Ruskin. Adrian Stokes's *The Stones of Rimini* and his book on Venice are useful companions to Pound's cantos on Sigismundo de Malatesta and on Venice's glory and decline. Richards's *Mencius on the Mind* is a useful corrective where Pound seems to be making the Confucian tradition too simple.

It is useful, also, to read the *Cantos* with a prose translation of the Odyssey and of Ovid's *Metamorphoses* handy; to have read an American muck-raking journalist like Lincoln Steffens; to have read Pound's own letters and Ford Madox Ford's various volumes of reminiscences, and Hone's biography of Yeats. It is worth also finding out what Major Douglas and Gesell really said. The more one has mastered at least part of Pound's material, the less puzzling at least some main lines of development in the *Cantos* will look; though there will always remain details to provide employment for young men doing Ph.D. theses. What would be very wrong would be to say, as some critics have said, that you can ignore the meaning and still get the poetry; Pound himself cares passionately for the meaning; and there are, indeed, many passages in the *Cantos* as dull (if you are not interested in the subject) as a school textbook.

Donald Carne-Ross, for instance, has pointed out that most of the names in the cantos on the history of China have no sort of reverberation, or resonance, for an English or American reader; in fairness to Pound, then, in such passages as these, you ought to read them alongside a short history of China. There is nothing *essentially* unpoetic in history which we do not happen to know; and there is nothing *essentially* poetic, either, in preserving our ignorance. A poet of the stature and of the gifts of Pound has the right, I think, to demand a certain amount of sheer hard work from us. The critic has the right, also, to ask how repaying in the end the work is. But my own feeling about the *Cantos* is that quite a number of passages which have not repaid me as poetry have repaid me by stimulating my curiosity; by making me look into things for myself. Curiosity, for Pound, is the quality without which the life of the mind, and the exercise of talent, wither away.

Something ought to be said about the narrative or connective method of the *Cantos*. Pound would not call that, himself, symbolic or allegorical. But, for instance, the very first canto is a translation of a Renaissance Latin version of the Odyssey, a version which Pound had earlier quoted in a prose essay on translators. The passage chosen for translation is that where Odysseus leaves Circe, digs a pit, sacrifices sheep, and calls up the shades of the dead to tell him whether he will get home or not, and how. The first ghost to appear is Elpenor, whom Odysseus left behind in Circe's palace; trying to join the other companions of Odysseus, but drunk and sleepy, Elpenor had tripped on a ladder and broken his neck. He begs Odysseus to set up some memorial of him. And Odysseus is told that he will return home, against the will of Neptune, but having lost all his companions (so, in his return

to America in 1945, it will prove with Pound). Now, the
raising of ghosts to ask them for advice is something with
which Pound is centrally concerned in this poem; the
temptations and bad luck which destroyed Elpenor
he sees as permanently besetting man in his quest for
civilisation; Odysseus is the type of his hero. But also,
approaching Homer through a Renaissance Latin translation, and making that alive in a style that sometimes
recalls Pound's own version of the Anglo-Saxon *Seafarer*,
Pound implicitly states the perpetual need for renewal of
our cultural heritage, and yet the need to base the effort
to renew on attempts at renewal in the past.

Similarly, the second canto is largely taken up with a
tale out of the *Metamorphoses*, about how pirates kid-
napped a young boy, intending to sell him as a slave, and
how Bacchus rescued him, filling the boat with leopards
and lynxes, and turning the wicked sailors into fish; then
the boy becomes a devotee of Bacchus; the story is told
in a very free adaptation of Ovid, with a slangy, almost
Hemingway use of dialogue, with brilliantly vivid visual
detail, and without any imitation of Ovidian point and
antithesis. Again, this is an example of making a tradition new, by drastically altering it in some ways. Bacchus
represents Pound's semi-paganism, his belief in the *deus
loci*, in a supernatural world very near to us in nature:
when he introduces the gods, for instance, he often also
introduces the Mediterranean sky or sea or landscapes
with olive trees, a sense of natural magic. The pirates in
Ovid, also, committing a cruel crime for the sake of
money, are in a sense types of the monetary criminals,
the arms-traffickers and usurers, with whom Pound will
be concerned in the later cantos. And the story is told,
as in Ovid, to King Pentheus to warn him not to be contemptuous of the gods; we are to take that warning too.

And the early introduction of the theme of meta-
morphosis (in several other examples also) should warn
us that we are going to hear all through in a sense the

"same" story but in "different" shapes. Adams, Jefferson, Confucius, Sigismundo de Malatesta, a variety of Chinese Emperors, Pound himself in the *Pisan Cantos*, Mussolini, will all in a sense "be" Odysseus; just as Eleanor of Aquitaine and Cunizza will be aspects of Circe. Similarly there are a number of women in the early cantos who suffer great misfortunes for love, Ignez da Castro, Parisina d'Este, and the girl out of Boccaccio who is given her lover's heart to eat, eats it, and jumps out of a window; they are all one. A supernatural power is upon them, Venus instead of Bacchus; and Venus herself is sometimes invoked as a deity.

Pound's gods are just as real in the context of the *Cantos* as his human figures, and should not be taken in any sense as mere "literary ornament." They represent, let us say, like Pan in *The Wind in the Willows*, or the old gods as revived by Richard Garnett or in some of the early short stories of E. M. Forster, or, more deeply, like Wordsworth's half-wish that he had been "a pagan suckled in a creed outworn," the longing of modern man to regain touch with the deep sources of life, however fierce and dangerous these may prove, however "immoral" by the standards of law-abiding urban civilisation. Pound has here something in common with D. H. Lawrence whom, on the whole, though admiring some of his poems, he very much dislikes; and something in common also, though nothing like such a learned mythographer, with Robert Graves, who very much dislikes him. He does not invoke a personal "high god," Jupiter or Jehovah; but he does frequently invoke a Neoplatonic image of the divine intelligence as mind or light. Mind, in a sense, for Pound *makes* the world: there is a strange, revealing phrase somewhere in *The Pisan Cantos*: "that the drama is wholly subjective."

Pound is a difficult poet in the *Cantos* for two reasons, and for two reasons only. He is very elliptical, he jumps from one thing to another, leaving the reader to fill in connexions or see relations for himself. And he always refers to any person, place, or episode he is talking about as if the reader were already familiar with it. He makes an unconscious equation of what he happens to know and what is or should be common knowledge. His digressiveness, his going off at a tangent, is sometimes mere wandering, mere free association; but in the first thirty cantos, at least, and in *The Pisan Cantos*, it is sometimes genuinely, in his own sense, ideogrammatic: two juxtaposed particular images, or episodes, apparently completely disparate, suddenly spark off a sense of a relationship between them; or a theme which has had little apparent significance when first introduced gains significance when brought in again in a different setting (this effect might be called fugal rather than ideogrammatic). As for the difficulty of his references, this can usually be cleared up by, say, a volume of Italian or American history or a textbook about economics or a dictionary of mythological figures or sometimes his own letters or essays. The meaning is always very clear once one has grasped *whom*, or *what*, he is talking about; he is not a difficult poet in the sense that Donne or Empson is difficult, he does not say abstruse or riddling or complicated things. Essentially, as Alfred Alvarez among others has suggested, he is, behind the formidable façade of learning, a simple-minded man.

But what can one say critically about the *Cantos*? Was the whole conception "wrong from the start"? Was it demanding too much of any possible reader? Was it a method of writing a long poem that could reach a climax or conclusion, or did it imply from the start an infinite expansibility? Would it be wisest to think of the *Cantos* perhaps not as a rival to *Paradise Lost* but to some sort of intimate journal (a journal primarily about the desire to write an epic, partly about three or four recurrent centres of interest, but loose and flexible enough to take in any bit of new material that came along)? The first thirty cantos seem to be a genuine aesthetic experiment; thereafter the interest gradually becomes less and less primarily aesthetic, more and more expository or didactic.

The long sections on China and on John Adams have a kind of poetic interest of their own, but it is much more, say, like that of one of Wordsworth's longer poems, demanding steady plodding from the reader, than it is like the kaleidoscopic dazzle of the first thirty cantos. And in *The Pisan Cantos* the form adapts itself, as not before, to a special kind of informal intimacy. Was it a triumph to have invented a form that could accommodate itself to so many different purposes? Or is the "form" of the *Cantos* not really a form at all but a pretext for preserving an identity, over years and over troubles, through unbroken self-expression? I incline myself, I think, to something like the last view; the coherence within incoherence, the obstinate sense of direction masked by wild distractability, of the *Cantos* is the coherence and sense of direction, perpetually threatened by chaos but perpetually also re-forming itself, of Pound's life-drive, of his mind. If we look at the *Cantos* in this way, even passages that seem failures, or of merely documentary interest, may well suddenly re-acquire for us the interest of art. Put this more simply: what the *Cantos* in the end are "about" is the isolated artist, and his struggle through an *idea* of tradition and community, towards sanity; what almost but not quite destroys the sanity of the artist, disrupts the organic being of the work, is the brutal failure of facts or "reality" to correspond to the "idea." When in the teeth of this failure of the world to be his idea of it, the artist clings to his idea, the clinging acquires a pathos, a dignity, a representative human value which the idea as such, unassaulted, might not have possessed.

So much for the general aesthetic problem. But even readers who consider the *Cantos* a momentous failure on the whole, would have to admit the presence in it, the frequent presence in the earlier cantos, of passages of masterly poetry: masterly above all in rhythm: from a rhythm enacting violence like this,

> One year floods rose,
> One year they fought in the snows,
> One year hail fell, breaking the trees and walls,
> Down there in the marsh they trapped him
> > in one year. . . . [46]

to one enacting serenity like this (it is Confucius speaking, in XIII):

> 'The blossoms of the apricot
> > blow from the east to the west,
> And I have tried to keep them from falling'.[47]

There is the rhythm of concentration

> > 'In the gloom the gold
> Gathers the light about it. . . .'[48]

(R. P. Blackmur has used these lines as the text for a whole sermon on how the gold of Pound's talent gathers the light about it in the gloom of his fate, his obstinacies and obsessions.) There is the extraordinary sustained delicacy of a passage like this:

> And of a later year,
> > pale in the wine-red algae,
> If you will lean over the rock,
> > the coral face under wave-tinge,
> Rose-paleness under water-shift,
> > Ileuthyeria, fair Dafne of sea-bords,
> The swimmer's arms turned to branches,
> Who will say in what year,
> > fleeing what band of tritons,
> The smooth brows, seen, and half seen,
> > now ivory stillness.[49]

Contrast the similar, and yet dissimilar, tone and rhythm of this:

And in the water, the almond-white swimmers,
The silvery water glazes the upturned nipple,
        As Poggio has remarked.[50]

There is a rhythm of elegy:

> 'Nor have they mound by sea-bord.
>   That saw never the olives under Spartha
> With the leaves green and then not green,
>   The click of light in their branches. . . .'[51]

There is demotic speech, with a kind of ballad or folk-
song quality:

> An' that man sweat blood
> to put through that railway,
> And what he ever get out of it?[52]

A passage like this seems to pad to and fro with the
frustration which its sense evokes:

> Time is the evil. Evil.
>   A day, and a day
> Walked the young Pedro baffled,
>   A day and a day
> After Ignez was murdered . . .[53]

Or another passage partly about Ignez but more about
mutability, time's caprices in ruining and preserving:

> Ignez da Castro murdered, and a wall
> Here stripped, here made to stand.
> Drear waste, the pigment flakes from the stone,
> Or plaster flakes, Mantegna painted the wall.
> Silk tatters, 'Nec Spe Nec Metu.'[54]

These fine lines incidentally are a very fine example of
how splendidly the "ideogrammatic" method can work,
when it does work. Without mentioning time, they create
the concept "The Triumph of Time"; and more com-
plexly, the sense that that triumph is not complete, that
somehow it is defied? How do they do this?

A collision of particulars, I think, sparks off a general perception. The murder of Ignez da Castro is the wanton destruction of young love and beauty. The wall that is stripped or propped has nothing to do with her story. It is the wall of a church, inside, either stripped of its "painted paradise," defaced by time's fell hand, or strengthened by restorers, as if by mere chance.

The stripping is like the murder. "Drear waste" applies to the contemplation of both them. We visualise a more particular wall, a fresco on it, with the pigment and plaster flaking away; nobody working against time's destructiveness, yet the fresco by a great artist, Mantegna. And then there is the image of the silk banner of some great Italian family with its arrogant motto, "Neither by hope nor by fear"; but the banner is in tatters. Yet the name of Ignez, the name of Mantegna, the insolence of "Nec Spe Nec Metu" still speak out a kind of defiance against time. This surely is great poetry, piercing clearly to some of our profoundest feelings, and great poetry using a manner of procedure of which Pound so far as I know is almost the inventor, and which nobody else certainly employs with equal skill: a manner of taking casual instances, and making them, masterfully, cohere.

I think there is enough "great poetry," fit to be set with this example, in the *Cantos* to make them permanently of major importance, even if we think that as major form they fail utterly. But the kind of major form they represent may be just this, a ruin perhaps, but a ruin that can teach us thus to ruminate:

> . . . a wall
> Here stripped, here made to stand.[55]

Pigment and plaster already flake from some of Pound's early poems. Perhaps many of the passages in the *Cantos* in which his conscious political and economic beliefs are most firmly expressed are like stripped walls. And to talk of Ignez da Castro murdered should remind

us that Pound is not one of these poets, much as he admires some of them, like Catullus and Donne and Yeats
and Graves, who know with tremendous tender and
agonising intimacy what love between men and women
is like; Yeats, so admiring and so generous about Pound
on the whole, once splenetically called him in a letter "a
sexless American professor." But there is enough major
achievement in the *Cantos*, I think, to make Pound deserve our reverence.

True poets are people ready to ruin themselves, and
what Robert Graves calls Muse poets are people ready
to ruin themselves for women. If Pound is not wholly
what Graves would call a Muse poet, he is not wholly
what Graves would call an Apollonian poet either. The
Muse poet, for Graves, writes for love, not for love of
art; he writes verse you learn by heart, not by rote. I have
a lot of Pound by heart. He has loved something desperately and ruinously, not just art I think in any cold
Parnassian sense, but *humanitas*.

I do not share the admiration, as I think I have said,
felt by a number of critics for Pound's later versions of
Chinese, his translations of the canonical odes; learning a
bit of Chinese has spoiled him there as a translator, I
think. His version of a play by Sophocles about the death
of Herakles has splendid vigour, but strikes me as being a
bit too much like Hemingway in the dialogue, like Swinburne in the choruses. His versions of the prose Confucian
classics, *Analects*, and *The Unwobbling Pivot*, strike me as
making Confucius a bit too much of a buddy, one of the
boys; just as in "The Ballad of the Goodly Fere" he made
Jesus Christ a kind of Y.M.C.A. youth leader. The little
squibs and parodies he contributed to Orage's *New
Age* under the name of "Alfred Venison" are first-rate,
hard-hitting comic-satirical verse of their kind, and, I
think, much underestimated. It remains, now, for me to
say something about his critical and general prose.

Pound as a poet is at once at times the most purely

aesthetic and at other times the most purely didactic of
modern poets. There is an old formula, that poetry
should delight, should move the feelings, and should
teach. Pound in a sense short-cuts or short-circuits between delighting and teaching. He is curiously unin-
terested in *moving*, in the nature of the feelings, his own
or other people's. One gets this sort of statement:

> One 'moves' the reader only by clarity. In depicting
> the emotions of the 'human heart' the durability of
> the writing depends on the exactitude.[56]

Or again:

> It does not matter whether the author desires the good
> of the race or acts merely from personal vanity . . . In
> proportion as his work is exact, i.e., true to human
> consciousness and to the nature of man, as it is exact in
> formulation of desire, so it is durable and so it is
> 'useful'. . . .[57]

Really pure aesthetics, one might paraphrase this, produces really pure didactics; and the business of moving
through having been moved, of learning to swim through
risking drowning ("In the destructive element immerse
. . . that is the thing") can be bypassed. So Pound's
criticism is sometimes brilliant at a technical level, the
craftsman talking about other craftsmen, and sometimes
also brilliant in relating the task of the writer to very
broad and high social ideals (hardly ever even aware,
however, of the need to relate that task to the complexity
of an actual situation, never at all ready to relate it to
shy, deep, and intimate personal feelings; he would be
embarrassed to talk about such feelings; and he cuts
through complexities like a Gordian knot). He goes bald-
headed for truth; but, as Donne remarked, truth sits on a
high and craggy hill, and if you want to get up to the top
you must go "about it and about." Pound, as a critic, has
never learnt the techniques of indirection. And I can

think of no English critic who has combined so many insights, so many discoveries, with so many instances, as it seems to me, of arrogance and fatuity. I can think, on the other hand, of few critics with more courage; few critics less caught up in any kind of "club" or "gang."

It is a brave critic's duty to risk making rash mistakes, not always to be looking over his shoulder, trying to catch the whispers in the Senior Common Room: Pound states this duty splendidly in an early essay, "The Serious Artist":

> And who is to judge? The critic, the receiver, however stupid and ignorant, must judge for himself. The only really vicious criticism is the academic criticism of those who make the grand abnegation, who refuse to say what they think, if they do think, and who quote accepted opinions . . . If they do not care enough for the heritage to have a personal conviction, then they have no licence to write.[58]

Pound has, in that sense, very much a licence to write. In an essay on Housman's famous Cambridge lecture, "The Name and Nature of Poetry," he writes:

> This volume reaches me with a friend's note that it has "upset a lot of the Cambridge critics." My first hope was, naturally, that the upset had occurred in the highest possible seas and at the furthest possible from any danger of rescue . . .[59]

He does not know what he is writing about. I. A. Richards came out of Housman's lecture feeling that Housman had put back the clock by thirty years; I do not imagine that F. R. Leavis, if he was there, enjoyed it much either. But a study of Richards's *Mencius on the Mind* might have improved Pound's versions of Confucius; and Leavis's chapter on Pound in *New Bearings in English Poetry* is the most concentratedly intelligent appreciation of *Mauberley*, in particular, in our language. Leavis also was very much punished (John Sparrow's little 1930's book on modern poetry, now out of print, reflects the rage he aroused) for intruding Eliot, Pound, Hopkins, Empson, into the academic scene. Pound does not know the score; but a critic can be forgiven this sort of gay wrongness when, like Pound, he has helped T. S. Eliot to get his earliest poems published; helped Eliot also to compose *The Waste Land*; helped Joyce to get *Ulysses* published; encouraged Yeats when Yeats was reaching out for his mature style; and, quite outside literature, been one of the first to appreciate the genius of Dolmetsch, Brancusi, Gaudier-Brzeska.

The great quality of Pound's criticism, apart from his extraordinary gift for spotting winners, is, I think, freshness. Anybody who teaches literature, or writes about it, for a living, knows how stale, how second-hand phrases, responses, and so on, become. Pound is always excited and alert as if he were seeing something for the first time; and he communicates that freshness to the reader. In his prose, as in his poetry, he "makes it new."

REFERENCES

1. Ezra Pound, *Personae: Collected Shorter Poems of Ezra Pound*, London 1952, p. 52.
2. *P.*, p. 52.
3. *P.*, p. 50.
4. *P.*, p. 84.
5. *P.*, p. 75.
6. *P.*, pp. 76–7.
7. T. S. Eliot, *Collected Poems 1909–35*, London 1936, p. 37.
8. *P.*, p. 24.
9. *P.*, p. 47.
10. *P.*, p. 93.
11. *P.*, p. 109.
12. *P.*, p. 108.
13. *P.*, p. 113.
14. *P.*, p. 113.
15. *P.*, p. 120.
16. *P.*, p. 119.
17. *P.*, p. 119.
18. *P.*, p. 118.
19. *P.*, p. 122.
20. *P.*, p. 147.
21. *P.*, p. 147.
22. *P.*, p. 146.
23. *P.*, pp. 78–9.
24. *P.*, p. 165.
25. *P.*, p. 167.
26. *P.*, p. 167.

27. *P.*, p. 168.
28. *P.*, pp. 168–9.
29. *P.*, p. 165.
30. *P.*, p. 197.
31. *P.*, p. 198.
32. *P.*, p. 200.
33. *P.*, p. 201.
34. *P.*, p. 201.
35. *P.*, p. 204.
36. *P.*, p. 204.
37. *P.*, p. 202.
38. *P.*, p. 205.
39. *P.*, p. 208.
40. *P.*, p. 209.
41. *P.*, p. 210.
42. *P.*, p. 210.
43. *P.*, p. 212.
44. *P.*, p. 217.
45. *P.*, p. 217.

46. *The Cantos of Ezra Pound*
    London 1954, p. 38.
47. *C.*, p. 64.
48. *C.*, p. 82.
49. *C.*, p. 13.
50. *C.*, p. 15.
51. *C.*, p. 98.
52. *C.*, p. 105.
53. *C.*, p. 152.
54. *C.*, p. 16.
55. *C.*, p. 16.
56. *The Literary Essays of Ezra
    Pound, edited with an intro-
    duction by T. S. Eliot,* Lon-
    don 1954, p. 22.
57. *L.E.*, p. 22.
58. *L.E.*, p. 56.
59. *L.E.*, p. 66.

CHAPTER III

POUND AND HIS CRITICS

Ezra Pound and T. S. Eliot have had more written
about them, in their own lifetimes, than any previous
poets in the English language one can think of. Of writers
more or less contemporary with them, also writing in
English, the three who compete with them in this respect
are James Joyce, D. H. Lawrence, and W. B. Yeats and a
good deal of the writing about these three is biographical;
a good deal, also, of the more elaborate expository or
appreciative writing dates from after their deaths. In
Pound's case, for instance, there is one book, Hugh
Kenner's, devoted to his work as a whole, at least three
books devoted to the *Cantos* and a volume of essays by
various hands on the same subject, there is a book of
essays and tributes collected by Peter Russell for Pound's
sixty-fifth birthday, and there is a little expository volume
on *Hugh Selwyn Mauberley*.

There is a book on the influence of Japan on Western
culture of which the liveliest parts are concerned with
what Pound and the Imagists generally learned from the
haiku. T. S. Eliot's introduction to the *Selected Poems* and
F. R. Leavis's pages on *Hugh Selwyn Mauberley* in *New
Bearings in English Poetry* are classically just and generous
fairly early appreciations of the poetry up to the *Cantos*.
Two close confrères of Pound's, Wyndham Lewis and
Yeats, wrote about him (Lewis in various places but
most importantly in his great book of literary-philo-
sophical polemical criticism, *Time and Western Man*,
Yeats most importantly in *The Oxford Book of Modern
Verse*) intimately, as equals; allowing themselves the

expression not only of admiration but of irritation, even exasperation.

This familiar intimacy of tone gives their criticism a special value which it seems to me that even that of Eliot (a younger man, in a sense a disciple, very much moved by the desire to express gratitude) does not quite possess. Joyce disliked Pound's political fieriness, and found the *Cantos* quite unreadable, as Pound found *Finnegan's Wake*. There are good essays on Pound by fellow poets a little younger like Allen Tate and R. P. Blackmur. Ronald Bottrall, in *Scrutiny*, in the early 1930's, had a fine essay on the first thirty Cantos. Donald Davie and A. Alvarez are two young English poets and critics who have written about Pound particularly well. The finest contemporary poet whose attitude to Pound has been consistently hostile and contemptuous is Robert Graves. Other critics who have expressed a pretty firm dislike of Pound include Raymond Mortimer, Sir Maurice Bowra, and Richard Aldington. One might, broadly, say that no contemporary poet has been more discussed and more disagreed about.

It is natural to attribute this disagreement among critics about the value of Pound's work to political or ideological disagreement. But I think this theory does not work. I am, for instance, myself an old-fashioned Pictish liberal, and yet I did a great deal from about 1945 onwards, when Pound was under a very dark cloud indeed, to see that he got fairly treated in English literary journals; and I know people who, sharing some of his more violent prejudices, detest his poetry. The disagreement also existed (not only between critics, but in a single critic's mind) long before Pound had involved himself, self-hurtingly, in politics. It existed, for instance, in the minds of Wyndham Lewis and of Yeats: I shall come to Yeats later: but some of Wyndham Lewis's passages, in *Time and Western Man*, seem to me to sum up in what is still a very vivid and contemporary way the mixed feelings which Pound's work arouses in any open, honest, and disinterested lover of fine literature.

Lewis was a violent and, no doubt, a cantankerous man. He was not an example of serene and easy balance. But still he was something as near as our century has produced to a Renaissance man: a painter, a critic of art and literature and philosophy, a writer of novels and stories and philosophical fantasies, a social theorist, a poet even, of surprisingly uneven and sometimes slapdash but sometimes superlative quality, a man, in short, in an old-fashioned term, of genius. His very lack of care for the ordinary social amenities and for the delicacies and reticences sometimes imposed by personal friendship, when a friend writes critically about a friend, help to give his purely critical work an extraordinary penetration and vigour. And he is penetrating and vigorous (though not, perhaps, finally just) in *Time and Western Man* about Pound.

Time and Western Man came out in 1927, rather more than ten years after Wyndham Lewis's collaboration with Pound in the *Blast* period. It has two chapters, Chapter IX, "Ezra Pound, etc." and Chapter XV, "A Man in Love With the Past," largely devoted to Pound. Their tone might be called one of affectionate exasperation (allowing that Lewis, perhaps, had not much of a natural gift for affection, and that for the brilliant expression of exasperation he had a very splendid gift, indeed). In Chapter IX, there is a preliminary tribute to Pound's generosity as a person. Lewis had turned to Pound, for money, for sympathy, for hospitality, in some time of trouble: he had got it: Pound was a "generous and graceful person" and "a kinder heart never lurked beneath a portentous exterior than is to be found in Ezra Pound." He goes on to say that Pound is not a "vulgar humbug" even in his "purely propagandist activities" but "a revolutionary simpleton."[1] He describes his collaboration with Pound on *Blast*:

That group was composed of people all very 'extremist' in their views. In the matter of fine art, as distinct from literature, it was their policy to admit no artist disposed to technical compromise, as they regarded it. . . . [Pound's] poetry to the mind of the more fanatical of the group was a series of pastiches . . . Its novelty consisted largely in the distance it went *back*, not *forward*; in archaism, not in new creation. That was how they regarded Pound's literary contributions. But this certain discrepancy between what Pound said —what he supported and held up as an example— and what he did, was striking enough to impress itself on anybody.[2]

In the same chapter, Lewis describes Pound as a "sensationalist half-impresario, half-poet." But Pound is being used mainly as a stick to beat other people. In Chapter XV of *Time and Western Man*, Pound is the main subject. I will try, renouncing the pleasure of quoting Lewis's magnificent punch-to-the-jaw, sadistic sergeant-major's prose, to summarise the argument. Pound, says Lewis, in his first paragraph, is not an originator, but a slave of fashion, and a parasite on originators; though there could not be a "cleaner and sweeter" parasite. He is similarly a parasite on the creators of the past.[3] Yet he is not a nobody; yet in a queer sense he is not a person either. There is nothing original about him. And, after all, one must quote:

He sees people and things as other people would see them; there is no direct contact between Ezra and an individual person or thing. Ezra is a crowd; a little crowd. People are seen by him only as types. There is the 'museum official', the 'norman cocotte', and so on. *By himself* he would seem to have neither any convictions nor eyes in his head. There is nothing that he intuits well, certainly never originally. Yet when he can get into the skin of somebody else, of power, he becomes a lion or a lynx. This sort of parasitism is with him phenomenal.[4]

Lewis goes on to say that if there were something basically false and unpleasant in Pound's nature, he would be "unable to enter into the renowned and noble creatures whom he has passed his time in entering"—for instance, the author of *The Seafarer*, Arnaut Daniel, Cavalcanti, Propertius. The genius in the host would detect any falsity in the parasite. But he sees Pound as a poet wholly concerned with the past: "He has never loved anything living as he has loved the dead."[5] Lewis obviously either never read, or never understood, *Hugh Selwyn Mauberley*. (What living person or thing, anyway, from Lewis's circlingly destructive point of vantage, his free captain's machine-gun post in no-man's-land swivelling round at both the entrenched armies, was worth loving? Lewis?) Lewis goes on to criticise, more technically, a quality in much of Pound's verse which he describes as a kind of "mock-bitter, sententious *terseness*," "a melodramatic, chopped 'bitter' tone suggested by the abrupt clipping and stopping to which he is addicted. It is the laconicism of the strong silent man."[6] And Lewis notes that this terseness is even more tiresome in Pound's prose than in his verse:

In his journalism, his terseness . . . is of a breezy and boisterous order. For example, such violent expressions as 'bunk, junk, spoof, mush, slush, tosh, bosh', are favourites with him; and he remains convinced that such over-specifically *manly* epithets are universally effective, in spite of all proof to the contrary.[6]

What worries Lewis more, however, is the terseness in the verse:

Were he a novelist, you would undoubtedly find the description 'He broke off' repeatedly used. In his verse he is always 'breaking off.' And he 'breaks off', indeed, as a rule, twice in every line.[6]

Lewis goes on to give technical examples of this from the early *Cantos*, examples which do not convince me of the justice of his hostile criticism (there is a sense in which one could say that Lewis had a coarse ear), but which are worth quoting as one of the very few examples I have found of detailed hostile *technical* criticism of Pound. He quotes this:

> Cave of Nerea
> She like a great shell curved,
> And the boat drawn without sound
> Without odour of ship-work,
> Nor bird-cry, nor any noise of wave moving,
> Nor splash of porpoise, nor any noise of wave moving,
> Within her cave, Nerea,
> She like a great shell curved.

These were Wyndham Lewis's strictures on this passage:

> This actually seems to belong to the repetitive hypnotic method of Miss Stein and Miss Loos [the great Gertrude Stein, Lewis means, and Anita Loos, the author of *Gentlemen Prefer Blondes*, a sweetly funny book to which Lewis had taken an irrational scunner]. 'She like a great shell curved' and 'any noise of wave moving', both repeated, are in any case swinburnian stage-properties. The whole passage with its abrupt, sententious pauses is unpleasantly reminiscent of the second-rate actor accustomed to take heavy and emotional parts. [May I remind the reader here of the little dialogue in another chapter, between myself and a young French girl, listening in to Pound's Third Programme broadcasts. "*Un comédien?*" "*Pas un comédien, un tragédien.*" *Anglice:* "An actor?" "Not an actor, a ham."][6]

Lewis goes on to quote some colloquial Americanese from the early *Cantos*, to this effect:

> He tried to pull me on Marx, and he told me
> About the 'romance of his business'. . So I sez:
> Waal haow is it you're over here, right off the Champs
> Elyza?
> And how can yew be here? Why dont the fellers at home
> Take it all off you?. . . .
> 'Oh' he sez 'I ain't had to rent any money . . .
> It's a long time since I had tew rent any money.'

Lewis comments on this, in his sharpest fashion:

> All Pound's comic reliefs speak the same tongue; they are all jocose and conduct their heavy german-american horseplay in the same personal argot of Pound. . . . Their thick facetiousness is of the rollicking slap-on-the-back order, suggesting another day and another scene than ours. . . . They are a caricature of Pound attempting to deal with real life—they are Pound at his worst.[7]

Lewis goes on to say, however, that the very failure of such passages proves the existence in Pound of an authentic *naïveté*. "And a simpleton is what we are left with. That natural and unvarnished, unassimilable, Pound, is the true child, which so many people in vain essay to be. But some inhibition has prevented him from getting that genuine naïf (which would have made him a poet) into his work. There, unfortunately, he always attitudinizes, frowns, struts, looks terribly knowing, 'breaks off', shows off, puffs himself out, and so obscures the really simple, charming creature that he is."[7]

Wyndham Lewis seems to me one of the very greatest critics of this century chiefly because he had this extraordinary gift of, as it were, transferring directly to the page (I imagine him as sitting by the typewriter with possibly a glass of whisky by his right hand) the blurted

and indiscreet conversational insights of an artist, to
artists, about artists. He is not an academic making
things clear to students, or a literary journalist being
polite at a party, or a lecturer to a lot of old ladies being
purring and condescending, but just a man, at once alert
and excited, amusing himself about equals, among equals.
I put these remarks of his first in this chapter, because it
is better, in any court case, to hear the evidence for the
prosecution before hearing the evidence of the defence,
and the summing up. And the manner is more genial
than brutal, after all; Lewis leaves us laughing at Pound,
but liking him.

And yet to call Lewis a great critic is not necessarily to
call him, in detail, a good critic. His genius as a critic was
to state, in an unforgettable fashion, the permanently
damaging things that could be said; as in the essay on
Faulkner, in *Men Without Art*, with the passage about
Faulkner's whip-poor-will machine, with which he pumps
magnolias and sourceless moonlight into his prose whenever, for lack of these dense, synthetic atmospherics, the
narrative seems to be flagging. He misses out, in *Time
and Western Man*, all Pound's greatest earlier achieve-
ments, *Cathay*, "Near Perigord," "Homage to Sextus
Propertius," *Hugh Selwyn Mauberley*; it is ridiculous to call
the author of these poems, or sets or sequences of poems,
in any really damaging sense (in any sense other than
that in which all genius has a terrifying simplicity) a
simpleton. The kind of attack which Lewis himself made,
in a splendid piece of rapid polemics like *The Doom of
Youth*, on the corruptions, fatuities, and sinister directions
of a journalistic-commercial culture, Pound does as art,
with the most lovely economy, in *Mauberley*. What Lewis
has done is simply, with brilliant tactlessness, to crystal-
lise, for ever, the most sympathetic reader's deliberately
suppressed doubts and reservations.

Yeats, the next major contemporary of Pound's whom
we are to consider as one of his critics, is not ordinarily

considered a very good critic of literature. Few readers, for instance, share his admiration for Dorothy Wellesley or W. J. Turner and it is only fairly recently that young-ish English critics like Frank Kermode and Iain Fletcher have begun to see what Yeats saw in, and what he learned from, his confrères of the 1890's, like Arthur Symons, Ernest Dowson, and Lionel Johnson. On the whole, though a wonderful piece of character-acting, Yeats's introduction to *The Oxford Book of Modern Verse* is a very eccentric critical document, indeed. A natural generosity of temperament (in this he was at the opposite pole from Wyndham Lewis), a dislike of wishing to appear the master of a school (he never liked the minor poets who imitated him), and a modesty, far deeper than his surface arrogance, that made him admire things that he could not do himself, all these conspired to make Yeats, as a critic, turn geese into swans. But here and there in this introduction, where he is able to combine admiration with a certain sense of personal detachment, he writes like a very great critic indeed. Thus, there are a couple of sentences about Housman and Hardy (the first is famous, but the second is even profounder criticism):

> The *Shropshire Lad* is worthy of its fame, but a mile further and all had been marsh. Thomas Hardy, though his work lacked technical accomplishment, made the necessary correlation through his mastery of the impersonal objective scene.[8]

And there is the unforgettable judgment on a lyric by Bridges:

> Every metaphor, every thought a commonplace, empti-ness everywhere, the whole magnificent.[9]

Where Pound was concerned, Yeats was admirably placed to bring into play this intermittent gift of his for penetrating and unforgettably just criticism. If the intro-duction to *The Oxford Book of Modern Verse* is, on the

whole, a critical curiosity, nevertheless the pages on
Pound are as memorable in their way as some of Coler-
idge's pages on Wordsworth. Yeats liked Pound, was
amused and sometimes irritated by him, admired him,
and owed him a certain debt of gratitude. At the same
time, he never wanted to write in Pound's manner, as he
wanted, for instance, to write in Turner's or Dorothy
Wellesley's; and Pound did not belong to the magical
inner circle of his friends. Unlike Synge and Lionel
Johnson and Augusta Gregory, Pound never comes into a
poem, is never transformed by Yeats into a heroic pro-
file. There were aspects of Pound, also, which stimulated
Yeats's wit, which is another name for his intelligence. His
own gift for creating complex form makes him sympathetic,
also, to the ambitious formal complexity of the *Cantos*:

> Ezra Pound has made flux his theme; plot, characteri-
> zation, logical discourse, seem to him abstractions un-
> suitable to a man of his generation. He is mid-way in
> an immense poem in *vers libre* called for the moment
> *The Cantos*, where the metamorphosis of Dionysus, the
> descent of Odysseus into Hades, repeat themselves in
> various disguises, always in association with some third
> that is not repeated. . . . Like other readers I discover
> at present merely exquisite or grotesque fragments . . .
> Can impressions that are in part visual, in part metri-
> cal, be related like the notes of a symphony; has the
> author been carried beyond reason by a theoretical
> conception? His belief in his own conception is so
> great that since the appearance of the first Canto I
> have tried to suspend judgement.[10]

Yeats, however, has not really suspended judgment.
The judgment in the next paragraph is the most magis-
terial general judgment on Pound that I know:

> When I consider his work as a whole I find more style
> than form; at moments more style, more deliberate

nobility and the means to convey it than in any contemporary poet known to me, but it is constantly
interrupted, broken, twisted into nothing by its direct
opposite, nervous obsession, nightmare, stammering
confusion; he is an economist, poet, politician, raging
at malignants with inexplicable characters and motives,
grotesque figures out of a child's book of beasts. This
loss of self-control, common among uneducated revo-
lutionists, is rare—Shelley had it in some degree—
among men of Ezra Pound's culture and erudition.
Style and its opposite can alternate, but form must be
full, sphere-like, single. Even where there is no inter-
ruption he is often content, if certain verses and lines
have style, to leave unbridged transitions, unexplained
ejaculations, that make his meaning unintelligible. . . .
Even where the style is sustained throughout one gets
an impression, especially when he is writing in *vers
libre*, that he has not got all the wine into the bowl, that
he is a brilliant improvisator translating at sight from
an unknown Greek masterpiece . . .[10]

Yeats seems to me to have hit in those passages both on
the central aesthetic problem about Pound's work (the
alternation of style and anti-style) and on some of the
psychological factors underlying it. It should be
noticed where he coincides with Wyndham Lewis.

For Lewis, Pound is essentially the child or the "revolutionary simpleton." For Yeats he resembles the "uneducated revolutionary" and rages at figures out of "a
child's book of beasts." The critical problem which they
both raise about Pound is not at all unlike the central
critical problem that people raise about Blake. Blake, too,
was a "child" and he might be described either as an
"uneducated revolutionary" or a "revolutionary simpleton." Blake's own crowning achievement, from his own
point of view, must have been the long prophetic books,
in which he managed to make a myth, coherent within

his own terms, of his unique and personal vision of the
world; the *Cantos* are a myth, coherent within its own
terms, of the same sort. But ordinary readers of Blake
prefer his short lyrics to the prophetic books; by the
ordinary reader, there, I mean the reader who is primarily a literary critic, not primarily a disciple of Blake's
ideas. Rather similarly, a first-rate literary critic like
F. R. Leavis sees *Mauberley* as Pound's crowning achievement; the *Cantos* on the whole repel and baffle him. A
critic, like Kathleen Raine, who sees the prophetic books
as Blake's crowning achievement accepts them also as a
sort of sacred book, a new bible; rather similarly, I think,
the critic who is quite whole-heartedly to accept the
Cantos must have wholeheartedly accepted, also, many
major elements in Pound's vision of the world. The stress,
particularly in the *Cantos* after the first thirty or so, is
more and more didactic, on teaching by examples. The
diction is often extremely prosaic or that of an exhorta-
tion. You must, if you are to persevere with this illustra-
tion of "ideas in action," have some faith (you must at
least assume a provisional one) in the soundness of the
ideas; Yeats and Wyndham Lewis though both, like
Pound, in a sense Men of the Right, see all the difficulties
involved in assuming, even provisionally, such a faith.

The third writer whom one can think of as an equal
who has written critically about Pound is T. S. Eliot. His
introduction to the volume of Pound's *Selected Poems*,
which Faber and Faber first brought out in 1928, is, even
among Eliot's critical writings, a model of tact and tone.
It was this introduction which first made me excited
about Pound, when I came across it as a schoolboy in
1931 or 1932. Eliot points out, first of all, that to follow
Pound's poetry from its beginnings makes the *Cantos*
much more comprehensible. He points out that *vers libre*
as, for instance, he himself wrote it in his early poems,
influenced by the Jacobean dramatists and by Laforgue,
and as Pound wrote it (influenced, for instance, though

Eliot does not say, by the *haiku* and experiments in translation from Latin, Chinese, and Anglo-Saxon) is not the
same sort of thing as the free verse of Whitman.

Eliot goes on to note the obvious influences on Pound's
earliest, non-free verse poetry, Browning, Yeats, the Pre-
Raphaelites, the 1890's. He makes the interesting point
that these masters taught Pound how to use the speaking
voice in verse, whereas it was, for instance, translating
from Provençal that taught him to sing. He notes the
paradox that people object to Pound both for being too
modernistic (in his form), and too old-fashioned (in his
subject-matter). But Pound's great and real originality
for Eliot is, like all true originality, a development of
tradition:

> Poets may be divided into those who develop tech-
> nique, those who imitate technique, and those who
> invent technique. When I say 'invent', I should use
> inverted commas, for invention would be irreproach-
> able if it were possible. 'Invention' is wrong only
> because it is impossible. I mean that the difference be-
> tween the 'development' and the 'sport' is, in poetry,
> a capital one. There are two kinds of 'sports' in poetry,
> in the floricultural sense. One is the imitation of de-
> velopment, and the other is the imitation of some Idea
> of originality. The former is commonplace, a waste
> product of civilization. The latter is contrary to life.
> The poem which is absolutely original is absolutely bad,
> it is, in the bad sense, 'subjective', with no relation to
> the world to which it appeals. . . . Now Pound's origi-
> nality is genuine in that his versification is a *logical*
> development of the verse of his English predecessors.
> Whitman's originality is both genuine and spurious.
> It is genuine in so far as it is a *logical* development of
> certain English prose; Whitman was a great prose
> writer. It is spurious in so far as Whitman asserted that
> his great prose was a new form of verse.[11]

The earlier part of this passage seems to me one of Eliot's really notable contributions to theoretical criticism, as worthy of fame, in its way, as (though less famous than) "the objective correlative" and "a certain dissociation of sensibility." The point about Whitman's free verse not being really verse, nor D. H. Lawrence's either, is developed in more detail by Sir Herbert Read in his essay on Pound in *The True Voice of Feeling*. Whitman and Lawrence, for Read, are writing biblical prose, with a rhetoric of parallelism; a similar interesting contemporary case is David Jones, the author of *The Anathemata* and *In Parenthesis*. Like Whitman and Lawrence, Jones is a man of genius, but it is more convenient to describe what he writes as liturgical prose, broken up on the page into convenient verse units, than as even very free verse. (I would tend also to agree with Saintsbury that the very long lines in some of Blake's prophetic books are really Biblical or Ossianic prose, and verse only by a kind of courtesy.)

It is the technical excellence of Eliot's essay which has led me into this technical digression. But it is not merely technical. Eliot notes, as Wyndham Lewis, too, had, that the specifically modern liveness of Pound's early poems is not necessarily to be found in his poems on twentieth-century themes: "His Bertrand de Born is much more living than his Mr. Hecatomb Styrax (*Moeurs Contemporaines*)."[12] He traces with beautiful subtlety the growth in Pound's work of the complete fusion of personal feeling and personal technique that we find in *Mauberley*. He points out how the advances in technical mastery, the advances in grasp of a personal tone, of original feeling, do not proceed step by step but, as it were, play leap-frog over each other. In a fine passage on *Cathay*, he praises Pound as "the inventor of Chinese poetry for our time." His translations seem "translucencies."[13] This will prove an illusion; in time they will be important mainly as magnificent specimens of twentieth-century poetry;

just as North's Plutarch is important mainly as a magnificent specimen of Tudor prose. Pound's originality is,
Eliot also rightly insists, as fully present in his translations
as in his original poems; and in his little squibs or
epigrams (Eliot does not distinguish these from *haiku*-like
poems) in *Lustra* as in longer or more ambitious-looking
pieces. He notes:

> Pound's epigrams and translations represent a rebel-
> lion against the romantic tradition which insists that a
> poet should be continually inspired, which allows the
> poet to present bad verse as poetry, but denies him the
> right to make good verse unless it can also be great
> poetry.[14]

At the end of the essay, developing an idea of which
he has already planted the germ, Eliot points out that
every good poet's work develops along two lines, towards
increasing technical excellence, and towards what one
might call (though this is not the phrase Eliot uses) a
mature grasp of experience. "Now and then the two lines
may converge at a high peak, so that we get a masterpiece."[14] Pound is peculiarly interesting in that his shorter
poems give us examples of (I am condensing Eliot, but I
hope not seriously misrepresenting him) form developing
rather in advance of mature feeling, mature feeling still
rather groping for an adequate form, and sometimes a
very close approximation of form and feeling. This, in the
early work, Eliot finds above all in *Mauberley*:

> It may give surprise that I attach so much importance
> to *Hugh Selwyn Mauberley*. This seems to me a great
> poem.

Eliot goes on to explain that the apparent "roughness and
naïveté" of the versification of *Mauberley* is the result of
"many years of hard work." But he appreciates *Mauberley*
not only for the "sophistication and the great variety of
the verse," but because it is a "positive document of sen-

sibility. It is compact of the experience of a certain man in a certain place at a certain time; and it is also a document of an epoch; it is genuine tragedy and comedy; and it is, in the best sense of Arnold's worn phrase, a 'criticism of life'."[15]

I have dealt at what may seem excessive length with these criticisms of Pound by Wyndham Lewis, Yeats, and Eliot, because they are criticisms by men of equal or comparable genius, and because they were the writings which, when I was myself a schoolboy or an undergraduate, first excited my own interest in Pound. Lewis's book came out in 1927, Eliot's essay in 1928, Yeats's anthology at the end of 1936. Of these three writers, Eliot was the only one likely to secure a respectful hearing for Pound in academic circles, or among, say, the Sunday reviewers; Lewis was a wild man; Yeats was greatly admired as a poet, but not taken very seriously as a critic. Even Eliot himself in the late 1920's and early 1930's was by no means the firmly established figure that he is today. I remember in my own undergraduate days at St Andrews in the 1930's that an interest in "this modern poetry" was rather severely frowned on; one was told to go back to the tradition of R. L. Stevenson and Andrew Lang. Things were better, no doubt, at Oxford and Cambridge, but there was still a strong entrenchment, in the English schools and elsewhere, of embattled conservatives. And when Dr F. R. Leavis of Downing College, Cambridge, published in 1932 *New Bearings in English Poetry*, with the central purpose of making (in particular) Pound, Hopkins, and Eliot academically viable, he was being very bold. He takes Eliot's introduction to *The Selected Poems* as the point of departure for his essay on Pound.

Leavis begins his essay by noticing that, in spite of Eliot's tributes to Pound as *il miglior fabbro*, "the influence of Mr Pound that can be observed from outside is secondary to Mr Eliot's." He thinks that Eliot's gratitude

to Pound has rather unhappily affected the tone of the
introduction. He suggests, rather brusquely or briskly,
that the fact that Pound's early work technically leads up
to *Mauberley* does not necessarily make the early work
interesting in itself. Why not start with *Mauberley* itself?
Leavis notes, like Eliot, the debt in the early work to the
1890's, Browning, the Pre-Raphaelites, but he is less
happy about it. Even the Browningesque handling of
Provence, in "Near Perigord," is "a form of evasion."[16]
The passion for translation bespeaks a certain amateur-
ishness, or the mood of the amateur, and even Pound's
modern themes are often mainly an occasion for verse
practice (one is reminded here of the remark of Wyndham
Lewis, whom, however, Leavis does not approve of or
admire, that Pound never, as a person, really *sees* anything). Pound's "dropping of archaisms and poeticisms,
and his use of modern speech-idiom, are particularly
interesting," but nobody, from the earlier poetry, could
have foreseen *Mauberley*:

> In *Mauberley* we feel a pressure of experience, an im-
> pulsion from deep within. The verse is extraordinarily
> subtle, and its subtlety is the subtlety of the sensibility
> that it expresses. No one would think here of distin-
> guishing the way of saying from the thing said. It is
> significant that the pressure seems to derive (we are
> reminded of Mr Yeats) from a recognition of bank-
> ruptcy, of a devoted life summed up in futility.[17]

This, which is indeed in some sense the central theme of
Mauberley, is hardly likely today to remind us of "Mr
Yeats"; it may have looked so in 1932, from Cambridge.

Leavis goes on to summarise some of the topics that
give *Mauberley* a "representative value," topics, for instance, like the shapelessness and drift of modern culture,
its lack of styles and standards; the isolation and the
"dubious status" of the artist; the obvious element of
something like autobiography in the poem, combined

with "the impersonality of great poetry," "complete detachment and control."[17] He then makes a kind of "run-
ning commentary" on the poem, noting the affinity
between some of the rhythms of the opening poem and
some of Eliot's in "A Song for Simeon":

> . . . it is not surprising that two poets, in the age that
> has been described, should have to learn to express so
> subtly by rhythmic means the break-down of rhythm.[18]

He notes, however, that in Pound's poetry there are
none of "Mr Eliot's complex intensities of concern about
soul and body":

> Mr Pound's main concern has always been art; he is,
> in the most serious sense of the word, an aesthete. It is
> that makes the peculiar nature of Mr Eliot's plea for
> the earlier work necessary. But here, in *Mauberley*,
> there is the pressure of personal experience . . . The
> poet is looking back on a life devoted to the cultivation
> of aesthetic fastidiousness, technical perfection, ex-
> quisite eclecticism. . . . What is the outcome? . . . The
> poems together form one poem, a representative ex-
> perience of life—tragedy, comedy, pathos and irony.
> And throughout there is a subtlety of tone, a com-
> plexity of attitude, such as we associate with seven-
> teenth-century wit.[19]

For those who think Pound's most important poem is
Mauberley, Dr Leavis's chapter on Pound in *New Bearings
in English Poetry* is the most important essay on Pound; he
has gone over the poem with a great economy of words,
but with such a thorough sensitiveness, that he leaves
subsequent critics nothing to do but expand him. It is
surprising, indeed, how much one writes about modern
poetry tends to be something that one has remembered
from this little book of Leavis's, without remembering
that one remembered it.

He is sharply doubtful about the *Cantos*. He quotes a

statement of Eliot's about the *Cantos* from an article called
"Isolated Superiority": "I know that Pound has a
scheme and a kind of philosophy behind it; it is quite
enough for me that he thinks he knows what he is doing;
I am glad that the philosophy is there, but I am not
interested in it."[20] He quotes also a critic who after
praising the *Cantos* highly suddenly turns on himself, or
on Pound, and says, "Throughout the book, he has sub-
stituted book-living for actual living." Leavis finds this
just and I am not aware that any of the subsequent *Cantos*
that have appeared, even *The Pisan Cantos* which have
certainly more than "book-living" behind them, have
led him to retract or qualify this verdict; but the point,
he explains, of this dismissal of the *Cantos* is to get a
proper emphasis put on *Mauberley*. The *Cantos*, he says,
are Pound's *The Ring and the Book*; perhaps that verdict,
now that so many critics and scholars are going back
with growing sympathy to long Victorian poems, sounds
a good deal less finally dismissive than it once did. Like
all the best critics of poetry, like Eliot also, for instance,
Leavis carries most conviction when he quotes. He has the
art of choosing a quotation that exactly illustrates sets of
qualities, or sets of defects, or balances of strength and
weakness, that he is talking about; he quotes nothing, in
New Bearings in English Poetry, from the *Cantos*.

Leavis's dislike of the *Cantos* might be connected, perhaps, with his dislike of *Paradise Lost* and, perhaps, more
widely of the epic style and intention generally. I have
found a good and sympathetic statement of Pound's
rather special, rather typically American epical inten-
tions in an article by Roy Harvey Pearce in *The Hudson
Review* for autumn, 1959. He connects Pound with two
earlier American poets, Joel Barlow, the author of *The
Columbiad*, and Walt Whitman. *The Columbiad* is, from
what Pearce quotes of it, a very bad poem, indeed, but it
is exciting to Pearce because of its typically American
utopian vision. Pearce quotes some lines of *The Columbiad*:

At this blest period, when the total race
Shall speak one language, and all truths embrace,
Instruction clear a speedier course shall find,
And open earlier on the infant mind,
No foreign terms shall cloud with barbarous rules
The dull unmeaning pageantry of schools;
Nor dark authority nor names unknown
Fill the learnt head with ignorance not its own;
But wisdom's eye with beams unclouded shine,
And simplest rules her native charms define;
One living language, one unborrowed dress
Her boldest flights, with fullest force express;
Triumphant virtue in the garb of truth
Win a pure passage to the heart of youth . . .

This vision of these naïve lines, Pearce suggests, is relevant
to what Whitman and to what in a different way Pound
have been trying to do; to create

a radically new kind of epic—an epic which, in its
very directness and overwhelming clarity, would have
not subordinated poetic to moral purpose but have
made them one . . . one which, lacking a traditional
hero in which to centre, would create him and make
the reader participate in that creation.[21]

He says of Whitman:

The end of *Song of Myself*, the moral object which syn-
chronizes with its poetic object, is to know that the
world is there, and in the knowing, to know itself as
there; in effect, through such a transaction to create
itself and the possibility for readers to create themselves.[22]

Pearce says also of Whitman:

He looks when he wills and interprets as he wills. There
is a dialectic here, but not a form. It is essential for the

H   E.P.

meaning of the poem that the dialectic be unique; for
the dialectic derives from the very motion of the pro-
tagonist's sensibility.[23]

Whitman has, for Pearce, a dialectic but no form. *The
Cantos* have neither dialectic nor form:

> rather [they consist] of decorously managed, ideo-
> grammatically set down instants of insight which are
> to force themselves beyond abstractness into the
> reader's conscious and so make him new. . . . If it is
> but done powerfully enough, there will be no longer a
> need to tell the tale. For it would be ours—ours in
> such a way that we would not have to have it told to us.
> As in Barlow's vision, and as in Whitman's practice,
> the end of poetry is that reconstitution of man which
> will entail the withering away of poetry.[24]

Pearce notes two things: firstly, that in this kind of epic,
in Pound as much as in Whitman, the poet is his own
hero, "as his epic is the struggle of his creative forces to
bring into being something which constitutes his central
subject." The author of such a kind of poetry cannot
afford to be critical and selective about himself. He forces
all his compulsions on the reader, Whitman his "homo-
sexuality and his political sentimentality"[25], Pound much
more disturbingly his "paranoia and anti-semitism."[26]
An indirect implication of this, though Pearce does not
bring it explicitly out, is that a poet of this kind, with this
perhaps megalomaniac or at least messianic ambition,
cannot fruitfully engage in intercourse with critics, with
critics in the proper sense of the word; Whitman would
have been unable to "use" Matthew Arnold, Pound, at
the stage of *The Cantos*, to "use" Dr Leavis. Instead, they
gather round them disciples and explicators, who often
express themselves with an embarrassing fulsomeness.
Pearce quotes a passage from a piece by Louise Myers, in
Pound Newsletter, 1955:

'It would seem that [Pound] has his fingers on the pulse of creation, and like the poet-philosopher Goethe, bequeaths more than he states: a myriad of facets of existence to be explored in coming years, an attempt to understand what this fire is that he . . . kindles in one.'[27]

We blush at such writing, Pearce suggests, and yet after all we are all looking for someone to kindle a fire in us. And, struggling as we all do, to find at least sometimes the "real hero" in *ourselves*, we can be taught and heartened, in an odd way, by the failures and weaknesses of Pound and Whitman, as well as by their strengths. We have our own failures and weaknesses, but we do sometimes "find" ourselves, as Whitman and Pound sometimes do. The writing of Whitman and Pound is as if the traditional hero of epic had been forced to write his own story and as if the writing, in an odd sense, had been the making; indeed, one comprehensible way of describing the *Cantos* is (though again, Pearce does not bring this out explicitly) to say that they are a very prolonged account of the occasions, in Pound's reading, his experiences of life and art and society, his loving and hating, his insights and bewilderments, that brought them into existence; the epic is, in a sense, about writing an epic; and Odysseus is Homer. Pearce's concluding remarks are:

I am reminded of some words of Robert Penn Warren in the prefatory note to *Brother to Dragons*: ". . . . if poetry is the little myth we make, history is the big myth we live, and in our living, constantly remake." The struggle to make the big myth into the little one— this is as good a definition as any of the American epic.[28]

Pearce seems to me to have provided as good a general account as exists of the special kind of charity we need if we are to read the *Cantos* with profit, and of the ways in which traditional definitions of what an epic is have to be

revised to fit the *Cantos*. What he does seem to bypass is
ordinary literary criticism. The wish, by a piece of sacred
writing, to recreate the self and the world, to make all new,
is a noble one, of course; but, of course, it has never
been achieved, even when sacred writings had led to the
foundations of churches or sects or communities. I once
had the job of revising, for Unesco, the English translation of portions from the sacred scriptures of the Sikhs,
the *Adi Granth*. I found these, like the *Cantos*, in places
noble and inspiring, in places pedestrian and boring;
there was a great deal of repetition, the same images, the
same key ideas, plugged in again and again. These
writings have created and they sustain a great religious
community, a community opposed to caste, idols, pil-
grimages, yogi, keen on good works and the family vir-
tues, but they have not, on the whole, transformed the
world or even India. One finds "literature" in them, but
it would seem pointless to judge them, as a whole, as
literature. Must one say something of the same sort about
the *Cantos* as a whole?

Let me take some hostile views of the *Cantos* as a whole,
held by some of Pound's fellow poets. In 1940, reviewing
Cantos LII–LXXL, those about China and early American
history, a fine poet and a brilliant reviewer, Louise Bogan,
wrote pettishly:

> The dullness and brutishness of the Ming and Manchu
> rulers described in the first section, are equalled only
> by the fustiness and mustiness of John Quincy Adams'
> [she means John Adams'] notations on life and busi-
> ness conditions with which Pound deals in the second.[29]

And she is pettish also, and I think unfair, about the
metrics:

> As for the metrics, they are often those of prose (which
> is a mixture of iambs, trochees, and spondees).[30]

Later, in 1948, reviewing *The Pisan Cantos*, Miss Bogan

was much more generous. On the *Cantos* as a whole, she
wrote:

> The poet was breaking down prejudices against for-
> gotten or neglected cultures. He was striking across the
> lines of specialist scholars, so strict and so snobbish in
> our own day. He was presenting the past as though it
> were all simultaneous and were still going on; he was
> making the point that in art this synchronization and
> timelessness actually exist.[31]

But she has this reservation to make:

> Pound's streak of charlatanry, in *The Cantos* as a whole,
> was so interwoven with valuable insight that it was
> fairly negligible. What became really annoying was his
> growing tendency towards obsession. The obsessed
> always lack that final ingredient of greatness, humility.
> They are also invariably bad-tempered and vitupera-
> tive. They hammer and scold.

But, like many critics who have strong reservations about
The Cantos as a whole, and in particular about the chunks
of summarised history, Miss Bogan is impressed by the
Pisan Cantos:

> Pound's imprisonment in Pisa seems to have brought
> him back to art and life. *The Pisan Cantos* shows a new
> sense of proportion. He begins to feel pity and grati-
> tude, and he begins to smile wryly, even at himself. I
> cannot think of any other record by an artist or a man
> of letters, in or out of prison, so filled with a combination
> of sharp day-to-day observation, erudition, and in-
> sight.[32]

The one notable poet who has been totally hostile all
along to Pound is Robert Graves. In *Modernist Poetry*,
which he wrote with Laura Riding in 1926, he described
Pound as "modernist only in the historical sense" but
conceded that some of his work, like that of Carl Sand-

burg, with whom he classed Pound, had at least "widened
the limits of reference, diction and construction in
poetry." He also devoted a furious paragraph to a tiny
squib of Pound's from *Lustra*:

PAPYRUS

Spring . . .
Too long . . .
Gongula . . .

When this, Graves wrote,

is seriously offered as a poem, there is some justifica-
tion of the plain reader and orthodox critic who
shrinks from anything that may be labelled 'modernist'
either in terms of condemnation or approbation. Who
or what is Gongula? Is it the name of a person? Of a
town? Of a musical instrument? Or is it the obsolete
botanical word meaning 'spores'? Or is it a mistake
for Gongora, the Spanish poet from whose name the
word 'gongorism' is formed, meaning an affected elegance of style? Is the poem a fragment from a real
papyrus? Or from an imaginary one? Or are these Mr
Pound's thoughts about either a real or imaginary
fragment? Or about spring seeming too long because
of the gongula of the papyrus-reeds? Rather than
answer any of these questions and be driven to the
shamefaced bluff of making much out of little, the
reader retires to safer ground. Better, he thinks, that
ten authentic poets should be left for posterity to discover than that one charlatan should be allowed to
steal into the Temple of Fame.[33]

This is a splendid piece of invective but, carried away,
perhaps, by temperamental antipathy (he met Pound
once in the 1920's and disliked him because "he was
plump, hunched, soft-spoken and ill-at-ease, with the
limpest of handshakes") Graves is surely making heavy
weather of what is a simple but rather good little joke.

The poem is the imaginary translation of an imaginary
papyrus, most of which has been torn away, so that we
have only the first word of each line. Gongula *must* be a
girl's name. The papyrus, if we had it complete, would
translate something like this:

> Spring (has come again).
> Too long (have I been away from thee),
> Gongula (my dearest).

The little joke is that simple love lyrics are monotonously
the same in any civilisation: "In the spring a young
man's fancy lightly turns to thoughts of love."

In the wonderfully readable Clark Lectures of 1955,
Graves was especially sharp on Pound's "sketchy education" and his lack of "an inkling of English tradition."
It is the English scholar and gentleman putting the half-
baked Yankee intruder in his place. Here is his most
slashing sentence about the *Cantos*:

> It is an extraordinary paradox that Pound's sprawling,
> ignorant, indecent, unmelodious, seldom metrical
> *Cantos*, embellished with esoteric Chinese ideographs
> —for all I know, they may have been traced from the
> nearest tea-chest—and with illiterate Greek, Latin,
> Spanish, and Provençal snippets (the Italian and
> French read all right to me, but I may be mistaken) are
> now compulsory in many ancient centres of learning.[34]

For Graves, in any case, Pound's ambition in the *Cantos*,
like Milton's in *Paradise Lost*, to write a "great" poem is a
mistake. It is enough to try to write good poetry, and
good poetry is inspired by love, not love of art; by the
Muse, not Apollo. And Pound is celebrating always
father-figures, Odysseus, Confucius, John Adams, Mussolini; he is the poet of a patriarchal conception of society,
the powers and energies which he thinks of as divine
emanations, light, intelligence, are traditionally associated with a Father God. For Graves, all Father God

religions are evil; Pound would therefore be wrong, in the *Cantos*, in treating Circe as merely an experience, a delay, a temptation. Pound, for Graves, would be celebrating mainly the insane pride of the male animal, his destructiveness, his herd instinct, his impossible wish for self-sufficiency apart from woman, on whom he ultimately depends. These two great poets are, in a sense, "mighty opposites," like Hamlet and Claudius; when I was young, and lonely, and sought above all things the male companionship of the tribe, my natural sympathy in this quarrel would have been with Pound; as I grow older, and my male friends drift away or repeat themselves, while my women friends are not only incurably loyal but always new in themselves and renewing to me, my feelings are more with Graves. The sand has shifted to the other half of the hour-glass. I think the future of civilisation depends, very largely indeed, on an enhanced prestige for women and the breaking down, which may be a cruel breaking down, of male self-sufficiency and self-conceit.

I have in this chapter confined myself to the consideration of writers who, as themselves creative, could in a sense speak of Pound as equals. I have ignored the work of enthusiastic disciples, patient expositors, political enemies, political friends. I have included one pure critic, F. R. Leavis, because his criticism at its best displays the same kind of intimate fusion of intelligence and sensibility that, with luck or grace, sometimes produces an important poem; and I have included Roy Harvey Pearce because he gives a very good general explanation of the nature of the *Cantos*. I should, I know, conclude with some brief statement on my own behalf. No poet of our time, or perhaps of any time, has combined greatness and vulnerability as Pound has. He can be seen, as probably by Eliot, as *the* major poet of our age; as by Leavis, as essentially the author of one very great poem, *Mauberley*; as by Yvor Winters, as an influential poet of the third rank, to be set, say, beside John Masefield; as by Robert Graves, as an impostor.

I think myself that he is an innovator of the utmost importance, a superlative verse technician, a poet with from the beginning to the end of his work an impeccable ear; an explorer of genius; a man bitterly and exactly sensitive to the pressures in a democratic society that kill instinctual life, rather as D. H. Lawrence was; a man, in all his personal relationships, of the utmost generosity of heart; a poet more splendidly and largely concerned than any poet of our time with the disparate yet similar essences of human civilisation; the poet, perhaps, as amateur cultural anthropologist. I think also that the great strength, and the great weakness, of all his writing stems from his Odyssean life, from having known so many men and cities, and having never really "belonged" anywhere; and from that, too, comes one of the vulnerable elements in him, the staginess, the show-off side. He has taken upon himself the history of the world, the wreck and the ancientness; crushed by this, but never losing the new voice of America. Ruin and failure and waning away are around him from his beginnings, but surmounting them, more importantly, the basic creative impulse and the basic creative power: "Make it new."

REFERENCES

1. Wyndham Lewis, *Time and Western Man*, 1927, p. 54.
2. *T.W.M.*, p. 55.
3. *T.W.M.*, p. 85.
4. *T.W.M.*, pp. 85–6.
5. *T.W.M.*, p. 87.
6. *T.W.M.*, pp. 88–9.
7. *T.W.M.*, pp. 89–90.
8. *The Oxford Book of Modern Verse*, edited by W. B. Yeats. London 1936. Introduction, p. xiii.
9. *O.M.V.*, p. xviii.
10. *O.M.V.*, pp. xxiii–xxiv, xxv.
11. Ezra Pound, *Selected Poems. Introduction by T. S. Eliot.* Faber paper-covered edition, 1959, pp. 9–10.

12. *S.P.*, p. 11.

13. *S.P.*, pp. 14, 15.

14. *S.P.*, p. 17.

15. *S.P.*, p. 20.

16. F. R. Leavis, *New Bearings in English Poetry*, 1932. New Edition, 1954, p. 136.

17. *N.B.E.P.*, p. 138.

18. *N.B.E.P.*, p. 140.

19. *N.B.E.P.*, p. 141.

20. *N.B.E.P.*, p. 152.

21. Roy Harvey Pearce, "Towards an American Epic," in *The Hudson Review* for autumn 1959, p. 365.

22. *H.R.*, p. 366.

23. *H.R.*, p. 366.

24. *H.R.*, p. 374.

25. *H.R.*, p. 376.

26. *H.R.*, p. 376.

27. *H.R.*, p. 377.

28. *H.R.*, p. 377.

29. Louise Bogan, *Selected Criticism*, London 1957, p. 179.

30. *S.C.*, p. 180.

31. *S.C.*, p. 182.

32. *S.C.*, p. 183.

33. Robert Graves, *The Common Asphodel: Collected Essays on Poetry, 1922–1949*. London 1949, pp. 137, 148.

34. Robert Graves, *The Crowning Privilege: The Clark Lectures, 1954–1955, also Various Essays on Poetry and Sixteen New Poems*, London 1956, p. 123.

BIBLIOGRAPHY

Note

In all cases in which more than one edition of any work are listed, all references in the text are to the edition marked * in this bibliography. The range of Pound's work in prose and verse, and as a translator, is so large, and the amount of commentary on it is also so large, that this bibliography cannot claim to be more than sketchy

I. WORKS BY EZRA POUND

1. Early Verse

A Lume Spento. Venice 1908. 100 copies on old paper.

A Quinzaine for this Yule. London 1908. Two hundred copies, first hundred printed by Pollock, second by Elkin Mathews.

Personae. London 1909. Elkin Mathews. Not to be confused with several later editions of collected poems, bearing same title.

Exultations. London 1909.

Provenca. Boston 1910. Selections from the above two volumes with some additional poems.

Canzoni. London 1911.

The Sonnets and Ballate of Guido Cavalcanti. Boston 1912; London 1912. Most of the London edn. was destroyed by fire.

Ripostes. London 1912; Boston 1913.

Personae and Exultations of Ezra Pound. London 1913. This also included poems from *Canzoni and Ripostes.*

Cathay. London 1915.

Lustre of Ezra Pound. London 1916. Reprints *Cathay.*

Quia pauper amavi. London 1918. The Egoist Press. Includes three "Cantos," some material in which was salvaged for the *Cantos* proper; and "Homage to Sextus Propertius."

Umbra. London 1920. A selective collection of the earlier poems.

Hugh Selwyn Mauberley. London 1920.

Poems 1918–1921. New York 1921. This included four drafts of early "Cantos."

Personae : The Collected Poems of Ezra Pound. New York 1926.

Selected Poems. *London, 1928. A selection from the above, with the addition of some early poems rejected by Pound, and with an introduction by T. S. Eliot. Page references here are to Fabers' paper-back reprint of *Selected Poems,* London 1959.

116 EZRA POUND

2. Later Verse

A Draft of the Cantos 17–27 of Ezra Pound. London 1928. Introduction by Gladys Hynes.
A Draft of XXX Cantos. Paris 1930.
A Draft of XXX Cantos. London 1933.
A Draft of Cantos XXI–LII. London 1935.
The Fifth Decad of Cantos. London 1937.
Cantos LII–LXXI. London 1940.
The Cantos of Ezra Pound. New York 1949. (All the pre-war *Cantos*, plus *The Pisan Cantos*.)
The Pisan Cantos. London 1949.
Seventy Cantos. London 1950.
Personae: The Collected Poems of Ezra Pound. New York 1950.
Personae: Collected Shorter Poems of Ezra Pound. *London 1952. This is substantially the same volume as the above, but there are some interesting variations, for instance, in the texts and line arrangements of "Homage to Sextus Propertius."
The Translations of Ezra Pound. London 1953.
The Cantos of Ezra Pound. * London, 1954. Substantially the same as the New York 1949 edn., but there are small textual variations.
Shih Ching: The Classic Anthology, defined by Confucius, Translated by Ezra Pound. New York 1955; London 1955.
Section Rock-Drill, 85–95 de los Cantares. New York 1956.
Rock Drill. London 1957.
Thrones. London 1960.

3. Original Prose

The Spirit of Romance: An Attempt to Define somewhat the Charm of the pre-Renaissance Literature of Latin Europe. London 1910; New York 1910.
Gaudier-Brzeska, a memoir. London 1916; New York 1916. Reissued London 1939. Useful on Pound's connexion with Wyndham Lewis's Vorticist movement.
Pavannes and Divisions. New York 1918. Essays.
Instigations. New York 1920. Essays.
The Collected Poems of Harry Crosby. Vol. 4, *Torchbearer . . .* , with Notes by Ezra Pound. Paris 1931. Limited edition.
How to Read. London 1931. This elicited from F. R. Leavis a reply, *How to Teach Reading: A Primer for Ezra Pound,* Cambridge (Eng.) 1933.
ABC of Economics. London 1933. Economics should be based on faith in the abundance of Nature and the zealous conservation of inherited skills.
ABC of Reading. London 1934.
Make it New. London 1934. New Haven 1935. Includes some of the best essays from *Pavannes and Divisions* and *Instigations.*

Social Credit: an Impact. London 1935. A pamphlet.

Jefferson and/or Mussolini. London 1935; New York 1935.

Pound's War-time Broadcasts. The Federal Communications Commission of the United States Government had transcripts made of Pound's short-wave broadcasts from Rome between 1941 and 1943: microfilms of these were made by the Library of Congress Photoduplication Service, Washington, in 1952.

If this be Treason. . . . Siena 1948. Four of the original drafts of the Rome broadcasts printed in Siena for Olga Rudge. Subjects: James Joyce, E. E. Cummings, Jean Cocteau, and a broadcast of one of the anti-Usura cantos, with explanatory comment.

Gold and Work. London 1951. This was the first of a number of translations published by Peter Russell of pamphlets on economic/political subjects first published by Pound in Italian during the Second World War in Venice, Rapallo, and Rome.

The Letters of Ezra Pound, 1907–1941, ed. D. D. Paige. New York 1950; London 1951.

Literary Essays of Ezra Pound, with an introduction by T. S. Eliot. *London 1954. Largely selected from *Make it New* and *Polite Essays.*

4. Editorial Work and Prose Translations

Active Anthology, ed. Ezra Pound. London 1933. The poets mostly duds; the preface interesting.

The Chinese Written Character as a Medium for Poetry, an Ars Poetica, by Ernest Fenollosa, with foreword and notes by Ezra Pound. London, 1936; New York, 1936. Pound had originally published Fenollosa's essay in *Instigations,* 1920. The essay and Pound's foreword are important in relation to the "ideogrammatic" method of the *Cantos.*

The Unwobbling Pivot and the Great Digest. New York 1947. Versions of Confucius.

II. OTHERS

BOGAN, LOUISE. *Selected Criticism,* here cited as *S.C.* London 1957.

Ezra Pound: A Collection of essays to be presented to Ezra Pound on his sixty-fifth Birthday, ed. Peter Russell. London and New York 1950.

ELIOT, T. S. *Ezra Pound: His Metric and His Poetry.* New York 1917. A pamphlet.

———. Introduction to *Selected Poems of Ezra Pound.* London 1928.

EMERY, CLARK. *Ideas into Action. A Study of Pound's Cantos.* Coral Gables (Florida) 1958.

KENNER, HUGH. *The Poetry of Ezra Pound.* Norfolk (Conn.) 1951; London 1951.

Leavis, F. R. Chapter on Pound in *New Bearings in English Poetry*, here cited as *N.B.E.P.* London 1932.

Lewis, Wyndham. *Time and Western Man*, here cited as *T.W.M.* London 1927.

Motive and Method in the Cantos of Ezra Pound, ed. Lewis Leary. New York 1954. Essays by Hugh Kenner, Guy Davenport, Sister M. Bernadette Quinn, O.S.F., and Forrest Read Jr.

Pearce, R. H. "Towards an American Epic," in *The Hudson Review*, here cited as *H.R.*, autumn 1959.

Yeats, W. B. Introduction to *The Oxford Book of Modern Verse*, here cited as *O.M.V.* London 1936.